Hypocrisy

Don't Leave Home Without It

Leonard Feinberg

HYPOCRISY: DON'T LEAVE HOME WITHOUT IT

Copyright © 2002 by Pilgrims' Process, Inc.

ISBN: 0-9710609-5-9

Library of Congress Control Number: 2002102540

Printed in the United States of America

0 9 8 7 6 5 4 3 2 1

Contents

The Nature of Hypocrisy

The Sources of Hypocrisy

Areas of Hypocrisy

The Ubiquity of Hypocrisy

One

Essence

I believe in this principle as a general rule, but it does not apply in this particular case.

One authoritative dictionary defines hypocrisy as an "act or practice of feigning to be what one is not; the false assumption of an appearance of virtue or religion; canting simulation of goodness." Another dictionary describes hypocrisy as "a semblance of having desirable or publicly approved attitudes, beliefs, principles, etc. that one does not actually possess." The word comes from the Greek *hypokrisis*, "playing a part on the stage, simulation, outward show."

Awareness of hypocrisy goes back a long way. In the Koran the word "hypocrite" appears thirty five times, in the Hebrew Bible thirteen, and in the New Testament twenty seven. The Hindu Bhagavat-Gita considers hypocrisy an unavoidable element in society, but the punishment promised in the Koran is not enticing: "The hypocrites will be in the lowest reaches of the fire." And Isaiah fulminates (9:17): "The Lord shall have no joy in their young men, neither shall have mercy on their fatherless and widows; for everyone is a hypocrite and an evildoer."

In the *Divine Comedy,* Dante assigns hypocrites to the eighth circle of hell, between embezzlers and thieves. In addition to enduring the expected inconveniences of the inferno, hypocrites are condemned to wear cloaks of lead. The eighth circle is near the center of hell, a location not generally recommended for comfort.

It is not only individuals who behave hypocritically. Entire groups of people—ranging from small aggregations to large institutions to great nations—practice hypocritical conduct. Garrett Hardin's definition of modern tribalism is useful: "Any group of people that perceives itself as a distinct group, and which is so perceived by the outside world, may be called a tribe. The group might be a race, as ordinarily defined, but it need not be; it can just as well be a religious sect, a practical group, or an occupational group. The essential characteristic of a tribe is that it should follow a double standard of morality—one kind of behavior for in-group relations, another for out-group."[1]

The key phrase is *double standard*. Everyone has observed situations in which someone says, "But this is different." Hypocrisy is essentially based upon double standards of behavior. When an individual applies the double standard he or she reasons: "I believe in this principle as a general rule, but it does not apply in this particular case." Or: "This principle is true. But it does not apply to me." That is also how group hypocrisy works. The group says, "This principle is correct. But it does not apply to us." Or: "This principle is correct. But it does not apply to us in this particular case."

All group hypocrisy is essentially the same kind of casuistry by which an individual convinces himself, or herself, that what he or she is doing is wrong for other people, but right in this instance. It is this kind of hypocrisy that a tobacco company practices when it continues to insist that there is no relationship between smoking cigarettes and developing lung cancer.

Russia pretended that its imperialist control of Eastern Europe was a form of democratic freedom. But in being hypocritical Russia is not unique. Long before the semi-perfect world was created by Moscow, a few non-Marxists also indulged in hypocritical deception. In the Hebrew Bible men like Laban made promises to prospective sons-in-law that they had no intention of keeping; men like Jacob tricked their brothers out of inheritances; and escapees from Egypt who worshipped a golden calf found euphemisms to excuse their behavior. Cain was less than frank about his altercation with Abel. And Eve, Adam, and the serpent were guilty of considerable pretense in their conversation with God after the fruit-eating episode.

Two

Individual

We are piloted in part by an ingenious capacity to deceive ourselves. . . . It is a simple step for the unconscious mind to act as a trickster, submitting to awareness a biased array of facts intended to persuade the aware part of the mind to go along with a given course of action.
—Daniel Goleman

Human beings use their minds to work, to study, and to rationalize—not necessarily in that order of frequency. In dictionaries the word "rationalizing" is defined as "To invent plausible explanations for acts, opinions, etc., that actually have other causes" and "To ascribe one's acts, opinions, etc. to causes that seem valid but actually are not the true, possibly unconscious causes."

Above the level of subsistence human beings seek satisfaction through ideas and illusions, some external (imbued by local customs and community values), some internal. Above the level of subsistence human happiness depends not on an objective state of reality but on what one believes, either as a result of one's conditioning or one's rejection of conditioning, is contentment. Everyone's happiness is determined by his or her concept of what happiness is.

One of the components of happiness is self-respect. But being a self-respecting individual is not easy; it requires continual demonstration of more courage than the average person is capable of maintaining. So rationalizing, to preserve one's self-respect, becomes an indispensable ingredient of life in society.

In the Orient, loss of "face" can be devastating, resulting in shame, violence, or suicide. Shakespeare said in Othello: "Good name in man and woman . . . is the immediate jewel of their souls: Who steals my purse steals trash . . . but he that filches from me my good name robs me of that which not enriches him, And makes me poor indeed." And Heinrich Heine was not deceived by facades: "You may depend on it: there is always a good reason if people are modest. . . . It is easy to forgive your enemies if you do not happen to possess sufficient wit to harm them, just as it is easy to keep from seducing women if you are blessed with too unsightly a nose."[1]

The human ego is so sensitive, so vulnerable, so allergic to criticism that it instantly fabricates justifications for its actions and concocts self-protective statements to explain its behavior.

The body protects itself against physical harm. Skin and mucous membranes prevent invasion of bacteria. The skin, in addition to providing a physical barrier, provides a number of agents that protect against minor challenges. If the barrier is broken and bacteria have invaded, a complex defense system goes into action. Circulating white blood cells, called phagocytes, aggregate about the invaders, and various chemical substances are released. One of these dilates the small vessels in the area, allowing more defensive material to arrive at the scene. Another substance calls for increased production of phagocytes and still another attracts the phagocytes to the proper place. Phagocytes engulf the bacteria and destroy them, using a variety of internal mechanisms.[2]

Another signal is received by the bone marrow, and lymphocytes are released that migrate to involved areas and release antibodies that further aid in the destruction of the invaders.

Many other remarkable procedures by which the body tries to help itself survive are being discovered. But it is not only physical attacks against which the body offers protection. Psychological threats also are resisted by a very complex system of internal defenses. Neuropeptides (chemical substances made and released by brain cells and certain other cells) bind to specific receptor sites in the body to convey information and control emotion. Recent research by biochemists and neurologists offers strong evidence that mind and body are inextricably interrelated.[3]

The mind is very selective in what it chooses to ignore. Neurologists have discovered a great deal about the processes by which the mind filters incoming information, blocking out disagreeable and disturbing items and facilitating the passage of pleasant and desired material.

The influence of the mind on the body can be measured. When the pupil of the eye sees pleasant things it dilates; when it looks at unpleasing objects it contracts. Experiments have shown that coins of the same size look bigger to poor children than to rich children. In *Human Behavior,* authors Berelson and Steiner attribute to human beings an enormous aptitude for distorting reality to satisfy their psychological needs. As a result, claim these writers, people tend to say what they think their associates want to hear, conform to group behavior, fantasize to escape unsatisfactory conditions, and use se-

mantic devices to describe reality in more gratifying terms than it deserves.

More than a century ago William James
wrote: "My experience is what I agree to attend
to. Only those items I notice shape my mind."
James assumed that this process of selection was
a conscious one. But ever since Freud, many
psychologists and psychiatrists have come to
believe that the mass of information coming
from the external world is filtered by the unconscious mind, which permits only a small
amount of the available information to reach the
conscious awareness of the individual. "Seeing,"
said Kenneth Burke, "is also a way of not seeing."

Psychiatrist Harry Stack Sullivan noticed
that the tendency to ignore what one does not
want to see appears very early. "Even before the
end of infancy," he wrote, "it is observable that
these unattainable objects come to be treated as
if they did not exist." The infant pretends that
the object it wanted has no existence—and since
it is non-existent, the infant has not been denied
what it desired.

Literally thousands of psychologists and
psychiatrists have delved into the phenomenon
of rationalization. But all of them, whether supportive of or antagonistic to Sigmund Freud,
begin with an examination of his theories. What
the Master said, briefly, is that all defense mecha-

nisms involve repression to some extent; all of them are methods of distorting reality to avoid pain. This distortion is not limited to deviant members of society. As Freud put it: "Much of this avoidance of what is distressing—this ostrich policy—is still to be seen in the normal mental life of adults."[4]

Although scientific proof of Freud's assumption (such as experiments with the neurophysiology of the sensory cortex) was not available until after his death, Freud knew that receiving a message and recording it are two separate functions within the human psyche. If the sensory signal that arrives is pleasant or neutral, it is permitted by the censoring element in the mind to reach awareness without any interference. But if the stimulus is a threatening or forbidden one, it is either blocked entirely or changed into a more acceptable communication. Freud suggested that two censors function during this process. The first censor prevents undesirable material from entering the "preconscious." The second censor, operating in the area between the preconscious and the conscious mind, catches the threatening elements that have evaded the first censor and had leaked into a location near the conscious mind.[5]

In *Vital Lies, Simple Truths: The Psychology of Self-Deception*, Dr. Daniel Goleman cites neurological research that shows how the mind handles external stimuli: "The cortex," writes Goleman, "the newest part of the human brain, expends much of its energy picking and choosing among this flood. . . ."[6]

The biochemical process that takes place when an individual is exposed to an undesired stimulus has been analyzed. According to Goleman,

> when an individual perceives an event as a stressor, the brain signals the hypothalamus to secrete a substance called CRF, or 'cortico-releasing factor.' CRF travels through a special gateway to the pituitary gland, where it triggers the release of ACTH (for adrenocorticotrophic hormone) and opioids, particularly the endomorphins. ....In sum, whether physical or mental in origin, pain registers in the brain via a system that can dampen its signals. In the brain's design the relief of pain is built into its perception.[7]

This technique for avoiding pain is a very useful tool for survival. The endomorphins help individuals save their energy for other tasks and other needs. Obviously, says Goleman, the kind of discomfort or threat modern people are most likely to face is not physical danger but psychological pressure. The hippocampus has adapted human responses so that a person can handle uncomfortable situations more easily.

In citing examples of distortion, Goleman points out that John Dean's "recollections" of

Nixon's praising him during the Watergate cover-up are not supported by any other source. "The ease with which we deny and dissemble—and deny and dissemble to ourselves that we have denied or dissembled—is remarkable," says Goleman. "But *the mind's design facilitates such self-deception.*"[8] (Italics added.)

We are all familiar with obvious rationalizing devices. All of us are more likely to take credit for our success than proclaim responsibility for failure. It is not unusual to hear university students say "We won" after a victory and "They lost" after a defeat.

Long before Sigmund Freud explained that dreams always mean something different from what they say, Joseph told the pharaoh of Egypt what his dreams really meant. Interpreters of dreams have existed for thousands of years, and today we are even informed of dreams shared by certain professions.

Modern psychiatrists claim that they understand the clues to dreams. Other people, or animals, in a dream, may—or may not—represent the dreamer's disguised traits. The time of day in a dream may—or may not—refer to a stage in the dreamer's life. The setting of a dream may—or may not—express alienation or freedom. Colors in a dream supposedly represent feelings. Symbols are complex metaphors. Dreams of falling suggest insecurity, dreams of being pursued express fear of our wild impulses, losing keys may—or may not—mean that the dreamer does not want to accept responsibility—or it means that the dreamer wants to be promiscuous.

But no one has explained satisfactorily why Nature deceives us in our dreams. No one has made clear why our psyche distorts the real wish, or the real fear, and presents it in the form of something else. It may be that Nature assumes we could not face our problems directly, or should not visualize our desires clearly. But even if the brain is protecting us by making the dream a pretense, Nature is guilty of deception.

If it is true that, through the process of evolution, Nature has facilitated the methods of self-deception by manipulating the human nervous system, an irreverent observer might suspect that Nature itself practices deception with a cunning that Macchiavelli might envy.

Three

Institutional

*The astonishing and perturbing suspicion
emerges that perhaps all that has passed for
social science, political economy, politics, and
ethics in the past may be brushed aside by future
generations as mainly rationalizing.*
— *James Harvey Robinson*

Institutions are as guilty of rationalizing as are individuals. Corporations, universities, political parties, social units, nations, and ethnic groups behave very much like individuals when it becomes advantageous "to ascribe their acts and opinions to causes that seem valid but actually are not the true causes." Imitating the subterfuges of individuals, the institution always pretends that the reasons for its behavior are nobler than they really are, and that the rationale for its position is more logical than it really is. Institutions, like individuals, almost never admit that their behavior is selfish or their philosophy self-serving. Although sophisticated business people defend "enlightened capitalism," and sincere communists stated that the state of totalitarianism was only an uncomfortable temporary phase on the way to ideal socialism, both antagonists were pretending. And institutions use the same devices for rationalizing that individuals use to salve their consciences and to maintain their illusions.

A century ago the Italian social theorist Vilfredo Pareto demonstrated that society rationalizes into dignity the defects of its institutions, exhibiting the same capacity for lying and indulging in the same vicious attacks on opponents that individuals practice. Institutions utilize the defects of adversaries, whenever those defects can help the competitive position or the public image of the institution.

James Harvey Robinson censured academicians for supporting the pretenses of institutions. "The social sciences," he wrote, "have continued even to our own day to be rationalizations of uncritically accepted beliefs and customs." He goes on in fairly strong terms.

> The astonishing and perturbing suspicion emerges that perhaps all that has passed for social science, political economy, politics, and ethics in the past may be brushed aside

by future generations as mainly rationalizing. . . . just as the various sciences of nature were, before the opening of the seven-
teenth century, largely masses of rationalizations to suit the religious sentiments of
that period.[1]

The more one knows about the actual operation of any institution, the more discrepan-
cies one finds between the public image of that
institution and the true condition prevailing
between the ideal and reality. Scholars have long
suspected, for example, that the religions of
ancient Greece and Rome were actually political cults. As Collins and Maskowski put it: "The
worship of Athena was the cult around which
clans united to form the city of Athens." Later
James Frazer would write in the same vein that
behind the lovely stories of love and jealousy
among Olympian gods was another religion of
sacrifice to the underground gods, sacrifice de-
signed to ensure fertility by magic means."[2]

Nietzsche, admittedly a biased commenta-
tor on the subject, said that madness is the exception in individuals but the rule in groups.
Freud thought that people in groups regress to
an infantile state. His daughter Anna believed
that defense mechanisms are "shared by individuals and families as well as by larger units."
And Robert Boles, an expert on group behavior, says that members of a group share a uni-
fied fantasy life.[3]

There is a characteristic of group behavior with which almost everyone is familiar. "Groupthink is a danger inherent in the structure of organizations," Goleman writes. "The success or failure of an employee depends to a large extent on his immediate superior's evaluation. This makes the junior employee more than happy to support the senior one's opinions." And this results in "two group tactics: rationalization and shared stereotypes."[4]

In addition to the rationalizing within the group itself, there is a need for institutions to play a role on the larger scene. An institution feels obligated to project an admirable public image and to defend that image, often by lying and distortion, when the institution is criticized.

Rationalization appears in institutions of all kinds, everywhere. In Africa, for example, Kung Bushmen of the Nyae Nyae area refer to themselves as "perfect" or "clean" and describe other Kung people as "strange" murderers.[5] The Mafia and General Motors, universities and churches, drug traders and patriotic organizations, all find reasons to justify their behavior, even when it results in deaths of drug users or the rejection of Black concert singers at a Washington venue. No one rationalizes more blatantly, or more loudly, than political parties, both in free societies and in totalitarian states. On the lighter side, that citadel of scientific medicine, the Mayo Clinic in Rochester, has no thirteenth floor. "If we did," a doctor explains, "some patients would not go there."

Nations who go to war rationalize; they never say that they are trying to extend their economic interest or their political power. No, it is to spread God's word or to bring civilization to barbarians that armies of strong countries invaded weaker ones in the past. And it is to bring freedom to downtrodden masses that the communist armies of Russia marched into Hungary and Czechoslovakia and East Germany and Afghanistan in recent years.

Like individuals, institutions resent criticism. And, like individuals, institutions fight back against critics by all means available, including lying, falsifying records, and persecution. Recently, a study was published concerning employees who made charges of corruption in the private corporations and government bureaucracies where they worked. The study showed that, although the charges were true, the institutions punished the whistle-blowers by "transfer, demotion, firing, blackballing, personal harassment, and intimidation."[6] The study revealed that the criticizing employees were not malcontents or political activists but men and women with long histories as good workers. They believed in their organizations and naively thought that all they had to do to eliminate corruption and inefficiency was to inform their superiors.

Most of the whistle-blowers learned their lesson. They now advise potential critics not to take action unless they are willing to risk their jobs and face continuous harassment. One complainant put it this way: "If you have God, the law, the press, and the facts on your side, you have a 50-50 chance of winning."

Like individuals, religious institutions do not like to be criticized, even by their own clergy. His satires kept Jonathan Swift from becoming a bishop in the Anglican Church in the eighteenth century, and it was his wit that prevented Sydney Smith from being made a bishop a century later.

When *LIFE* magazine was flourishing it avoided the restriction on pictures of nude women by reproducing many of the world's great paintings that happened to feature nudes. When the law in England forbade the use of moving nudes, English producers placed on stage attractive naked women who remained motionless.

There is a charming rationalization in India's anecdote about the creation. When God first experimented with making man, He put a clay figure into the kiln. But He pulled it out too soon, and the figure came out colored white. God tried again, but He was interrupted during the firing and by the time He belatedly took the figure out of the kiln it was black. So God tried once more. This time He gauged the process carefully and achieved the perfect result— a brown man.

Like individuals, institutions must rationalize. Just as individuals excuse their failures or account for their misfortunes by blaming them on other persons or groups, so institutions blame their failures and misfortunes on competitors or other institutions. They do not explain why these other institutions, facing the same problems they do, manage to succeed. Hypocrisy, rationalizing, pretense of nobility and altruism, are characteristic of all institutions in varying degrees. Even a Tory like Samuel Johnson wrote, "Patriotism is the last refuge of the scoundrel."

It is generally agreed that prejudice by Whites against Blacks, or Blacks against Whites, is an undesirable attitude. But there is ample evidence of White prejudice against Whites and Black prejudice against Blacks. The history of Europe bears sufficient proof of the former. And there is no lack of testimony for the discrimination of Blacks against Blacks and against other colors. In recent years Black governments have driven Asian persons out of residence and occupation in African countries. Blacks in Zanzibar massacred their long-time Arab neighbors in the 1960s. Arabs in Sudan massacred and expelled Blacks in Sudan's southern region. In many parts of Black Africa, tribal rivalries have flared. The bloody Nigerian war against Biafra's secession was only one conspicuous example. Ghana has driven out Nigerian settlers and Nigeria expels Ghanaians. In many of the African countries that were recently freed from colonial control, tribes have slaughtered other tribes as ferociously and indiscriminately as White rulers did in the past.

The prejudice of one racial group against another is heinous, of course. Every nation says so, and every nation is guilty of racial prejudice within its borders and beyond them. Some of these examples are abominable. Other instances amusingly illustrate this hypocrisy. The Japanese agree that white discrimination against blacks is odious behavior; but it is all right in Japan to discriminate against Koreans. In a professional baseball game in Tokyo, a Korean player, tired of racial insults by the crowd, went after a scurrilous fan with a bat. Jackie Robinson would have sympathized with him.

Racial prejudice is reprehensible. But a news story in *The Des Moines Register* revealed that even "a simple drawing of a smiling face—a popular symbol of friendliness on buttons, bumper stickers, and T-shirts—can take on an unfriendly meaning in Iowa City." The "smile" symbol, when drawn on listings at a rental agency, meant that the landlord didn't want his property shown to Blacks. Code words have been used in other cities to keep undesired people out. "In Cedar Rapids, the phrase 'nice people' written on forms was translated to mean no Blacks. The phrase 'good people' meant 'no hippie types.'" And in Waterloo, "if the date on the application was written out in full, it meant the landlord did not want Black tenants. Otherwise, the date would be written in numbers only."

Hypocrisy may take the form of class discrimination. The Dutch, proud of their reputation for social equality, conceal the fact that *Jonkheers* and *Jonkvrows* (descendants of minor nobility) try to marry only members of their own social class and urge their children to do likewise. The Japanese do not admit the existence of a "fourth class," descendants of medieval dirty-job laborers, whom proper Japanese do not marry or associate with.

Sometimes institutional hypocrisy becomes patently ridiculous. The *Agence France-Presse* reported from South Africa: "Petty apartheid has become pet apartheid in Cape Town, as dogs and cats belonging to non-Whites have been refused boarding facilities at the Society for Prevention to Cruelty to Animals kennels, reserved for the pets of Whites." And in 1972 the South

African Federation Cup Tennis Tournament permitted Black players to participate if they wore
badges that made them "honorary Whites."

But capitalistic bureaucracies do not have a
monopoly on obvious hypocrisy. A Soviet humor magazine ran the following cartoon: A
young Russian bureaucrat with a briefcase
rushes into the office, five minutes late. His boss,
crossword puzzle in hand, is angrily pointing
to the clock. Also glaring at him are his co-work-
ers who are playing chess, knitting, and having
coffee.

Unpleasant facts, painful communications,
and shameful knowledge disturb the self-es-
teem of the individual, the family, the group,
and the nation. The easiest way to deal with undesired information is to ignore it, to pretend
that it does not exist. In the past, rulers killed
messengers who brought bad news; today it is
easier to ignore their messages.

Four

General

The notion that we can transfer our guilt and sufferings to some other being who will bear them for us is familiar to the savage mind.
— *Sir James Frazer*

The use of scapegoats is one kind of rationalizing. An early example is vividly described in the Bible (Lev. 16:21):"And Aaron shall lay both his hands upon the head of the live goat, and confess over him all the iniquities of the children of Israel, and all their transgressions in all their sins, putting them upon the head of the goat." This Biblical scapegoat was more fortunate than its successors; it was led away into the wilderness and permitted to go free.

But later scapegoats, and, ironically, the Jews themselves, were treated much worse. James Frazer and other anthropologists have identified a number of animals and human beings who were forced to suffer or die as unwilling substitutes for others. In many early cultures innocent human beings were selected to die in place of local royalty, or to serve as sacrificial expiation for group sins or group misfortune. Scapegoats are rarely used today in this ritualistic manner. But all over the world, every day, individual human beings are unfairly blamed by other persons for the failures and misfortunes of the latter.

The dictionary definition of "scapegoat" is succinct: "A person made to bear the blame for others or to suffer in their place." The tendency to blame others for our own misfortune is a universal form of rationalization. And this form of rationalization results in vicious examples of hypocrisy. "Unable to beat the Indians," says a Burmese proverb, "he attacks the Akanese."

James Frazer described the process in *The Golden Bough.*

> The notion that we can transfer our guilt and sufferings to some other being who will bear them for us is familiar to the savage mind. . . . Because it is possible to shift a load of wood, stones, or what not, from our own back to the back of another, the savage fancies that it is equally possible to shift

> the burden of his pains and sorrows to an-
> other, who will suffer them in his stead.
> Upon this idea he acts, and the result is an
> endless number of very unamiable devices
> for palming off on someone else the trouble
> that a man shrinks from bearing himself.
> In short, the principle of vicarious suffer-
> ing is commonly understood and practiced
> by races who stand on a low level of social
> and intellectual culture.[1]

Sir James must have known that the use of the scapegoat is not limited to races on a low level of intellectual culture.

A three-line poem called a *senryu* shows that the Japanese are familiar with the scapegoat concept.

> The hanger-on
> Goes next door
> To get angry.

Psychologists agree that neurotic symptoms originate as defenses against anxiety. In the most common phobias, to conceal distress that is so disturbing that it cannot be acknowledged, individuals develop irrational aversions to persons, objects, or actions that are unconnected with their anxiety. On a larger scale, for the same reasons, institutions, tribal groups, and nations also develop unreasonable animosity towards individuals and groups unrelated to their problems.

Nor are human beings the only creatures who vent their frustrations on scapegoats.

Konrad Lorenz observed so many examples of "redirected activity" in the animal kingdom that he wrote his book *On Aggression*. When the male cichlid fish becomes angry with his mate, he charges to ram her, as in fighting. "He actually launches a furious attack which, however, is not directed at his mate but, passing her narrowly, finds its goal in another member of his species. Under natural conditions this is regularly the territorial neighbor."[2] Lorenz compares the fish's behavior to that of a man who, angry with another man, hits the table instead of the other man's jaw. "Most of the known cases of redirected activity," writes Lorenz, "concern aggressive behavior elicited by an object that simultaneously evokes fear. . . . The animal vents its anger on some innocent bystander or even on some inanimate substitute object."[3]

Lorenz considers the behavior of the cichlid fish more chivalrous than the analogous behavior of the human male who, "angry with his employer during the day, discharges this pent-up irritation on his unfortunate wife in the evening."[4]

So there it is—another form of rationalization that results in hypocrisy. We no longer practice ancient rituals such as Inca drownings of virgin maidens to appease the gods or the old custom of choosing a handsome young man who lived like a prince for a year and was then killed as a sacrifice to a vengeful god. But today the use of scapegoats is more wide-spread than ever: the slaughter of innocent people in the Catholic-Protestant conflict of Northern Ireland, Arab-Israeli hostility, Hindu-Moslem and Hindu-Sikh riots of India, Buddhist-Hindu atrocities of Sri Lanka, and Christian-Moslem murders in Lebanon. And in the peaceful everyday life of other nations, the persecution of scapegoats goes on more quietly, but continuously.

A popular delusion states "You shall know the truth and the truth will make you free." A more accurate description of human behavior would state, "You shall believe those truths and those falsehoods that make you happy." Fantasies are indispensable to human beings. Whether the delusion promises joy in heaven or happiness under a particular political system in this life, people need gratifying illusions to make existence more bearable.

As a general rule, human beings prefer pleasant falsehoods to unpleasant truths. In *Brideshead Revisited* Evelyn Waugh has a character say, "'I have left behind illusion,' I said to myself. 'Henceforth I live in a world of three dimensions—with the aid of my five senses.' I have since learned that there is no such world."

The argument between those who idealize man's nature and those who demean it has gone on for a very long time and is not likely to be resolved now. In a defense of cynicism Rich Dawkins writes, "We are survival machines—robot vehicles blindly programmed to preserve the selfish molecules known to us as genes."[5] But both cynics and idealists try to rationalize away the inconsistencies in their simplistic philosophies.

Rationalizing takes many forms. Certainly most of the great villains of history did not consider themselves villains and did not feel guilty. From Genghis Khan to J. Paul Getty, from the Huns to Hitler, from Tamerlane to modern gangsters, these people had—and have—a self-image as satisfying as that of the ordinary citizen and they enjoyed life as much as—or more than—virtuous human beings. And thousands of modern intellectuals compartmentalize their minds to make room for both contemporary science and archaic religion.

In a book called *Excuses: Masquerades in Search of Grace,* psychologist Charles R. Snyder concludes that there are three basic types of excuses: 1) "I didn't do it." 2) "It wasn't so bad." 3) "Yes, but ..." Professor Snyder estimates that many Americans use these excuses to a disturbing degree.

Excuses, of course, are a variant of rationalization. And most human beings often make promises that they have no intention of keeping, although they sometimes convince themselves that they mean what they say when they say it.

Another common rationalization, for people who have failed to attain a material objective such as wealth, success in their profession, or social status, is to tell themselves that it is only non-material things that are important—and that it is these things on which they will concentrate. Which may be true. Unfortunately, most of these people are not temperamentally suited to focus on spiritual objectives and they soon give up trying. Or, like Baudelaire, they go on suffering.

One reason why people rationalize so much is that most people really like much of what formal education tells them they should despise, and they don't really want much of what intellectuals tell them they should admire—such as the fine arts and "culture." So they pay lip-service to aesthetics and the higher morality, and do what they want to do in everyday life.

In the fairy tale of the three little pigs, the wolf huffed and puffed until he blew down the straw house. If the pig who had built that house blamed its inadequacy on the color of the straw, he would be doing what political parties do after losing elections, corporations do after going bankrupt, and defeated athletes do after losing. Human beings rationalize away their frustrations, redirecting them at neighbors, outsiders, the weather, the position of the stars, and just about everything else they can think of.

Even when they are functioning below normal capacity, people tend to rationalize. The woman producing an amateur play phoned a man who had expressed interest in trying out for a part. The man was so drunk he could barely communicate, but he told the producer, "Call me some other time when you're feeling better."

Stephen Crane's poem is apropos:
> I saw a man pursuing the horizon;
> Round and round they sped.
> I was disturbed at this;
> I accosted the man.
> 'It is futile,' I said,
> 'You can never—'
> 'You lie,' he cried,
> And ran on.

Sometimes there is a tremendous discrepancy between illusion and reality. But for the conduct of everyday life, the validity of what one believes is less important than the fact that one believes in something comforting. One might say, taking a quick look below the surface of life, that the motto for most human beings has always been: You shall know a comforting falsehood and it will make you happy.

Five

Philosophical

*Both Freud and Jung seem to have built into
their theories and writings a conception and an
interpretation of their own personalities.*
—Charles Rycroft

Every philosopher creates or adopts a philosophy that supports the needs of his or her own temperament. Every philosopher concocts a philosophy to match the accidental experiences that he or she had undergone. The process of developing a philosophy does not consist of selecting impartially from all conceivable philosophic positions the one that seems logically to be the correct one. Instead, what happens is that every philosopher, unconsciously or intentionally, constructs a set of arguments that prop up the emotional, psychological, and physical needs of the person who is concocting the philosophy. As James Harvey Robinson wrote, "Our so-called reasoning consists in finding arguments for going on believing as we already do."[1]

Reason always manages to find rational justification for emotional behavior. Plato was satisfying Plato's needs when he fabricated "idealism"; Hobbes was responding to Hobbes' requirements when he defended "materialism"; and Nietzche reacted to Nietzche's violent swings of mood when he spouted Nietzcheism.

But philosophers are not the only ones who rationalize in this way. All human beings do the same thing. To the extent that every person has a "philosophy," that philosophy matches his or her personality and experience. There is nothing new in this suggestion, although the proponents of this belief do not agree on the explanation of the phenomenon. Their analyses vary.

For example, psychiatrist Alfred Adler insisted that all the roles that human beings play in their social relations are compensations for their inferiority. (Adler himself was only five feet three inches tall.) Political scientist Harold Lasswell suggests that politicians work out their personal problems in the political doctrines they espouse. Sociobiologist Edward Wilson agrees; ethical philosophers, he is convinced, determine universal standards of morality "by consulting the emotive centers of their own hypothalamic-limbic system. This is also true of the developmentalists, even when they are being their most severely objective."[2] And criticizing what he considers the unscientific views of certain psycholinguists, Wilson charges: "Like poet naturalists, the structuralists celebrate idiosyncratic personal visions."[3]

André Gide also doubted that men and women unconstrainedly choose the beliefs they hold. "The trouble with most people," he wrote, "is that they think they have freely accepted or chosen the opinions they profess, which are actually as predetermined and ordained as the color of their hair or the odor of their breath."[4] In *The Private Life of Helen of Troy,* John Erskine has Agamemnon say to Menelaos: "Our special philosophies, brother, are evolved that we may live peaceably with our own past."

In every society there are "risk takers," entrepreneurs, and innovators whose genetic needs are very different from those of the timid majority. These danger-loving individuals evolve a philosophy that justifies thrill-seeking and change as indispensable ingredients of social development.

Other attempts at explaining human behavior offer a great variety of approaches. Find a person's heroes or heroines, says William Bolitho, find the individuals he admired in history or contemporary society, or the characters he idolized in literature or films, and you will get an insight into his motivation. (The implication, of course, is that the people we choose to emulate are somehow similar to ourselves in temperament, so that whether we choose a Napoleon or a Francis of Assisi to imitate, we are responding to an unconscious recognition of affinity.)

In many ways the personal predilections of individuals reveal themselves in supposedly objective choices. A study of leading American social psychologists concludes that out of twelve scholars who claim that environment is more important, eleven are liberals; of twelve scholars who insist that heredity is more significant, eleven are conservative.

What most intelligent people achieve is a convincing logical refutation of beliefs with which they disagree. They do not formulate a positive system of belief that is valid for other temperaments than their own. Brilliant intellectuals demonstrate an incredible ingenuity in supporting their psychological needs and pretending that an objective rational argument is being made. At the same time other brilliant intellectuals support antithetical psychological needs and pretend that they are being objective. And, pretending that it is absolute truth they are expressing, fanatics support their psychological needs with a passion that can be frightening.

Thomas More's martyrdom does not prove the validity of Catholicism any more than the martyrdom of a communist proves the validity of Marxism. It does suggest that both men were temperamentally inclined toward absolutism. The history of society shows that all major controversies, in philosophy and the arts and the social sciences, have been equally well argued by opposing theorists. These theoreticians defended what their temperaments forced them to defend, and they attacked what their personalities forced them to attack. Like them, we choose from the available beliefs those that please or comfort us. Everyone needs a primary belief to live by, preferably one that is not too obviously absurd. Happiness consists of finding such an belief and retaining it.

If it is true that people develop philosophies to match their temperaments and experiences, then individuals with similar personalities and experiences should concoct roughly similar views of the world. And persons who suffer from various aberrations should evolve expressions of belief that fit those deviations.

The most popular diagnoses of personality in the twentieth century involve neuroticism. Certainly the great psychoanalysts were aware of their own neuroses. Marcel Proust went so far as to write,

> Everything great in the world comes from neurotics. They alone have founded our re-

> ligions and composed our masterpieces. . .
> We enjoy lovely music, beautiful paintings,
> a thousand intellectual delicacies, but we
> have no idea of their cost, to those who in-
> vented them, in sleepless nights, tears . . .
> and the fear of death, which is worse than
> all the rest.[5]

Proust was neurotic enough himself to appreciate how much his world-view was determined by his personal maladjustment. Maurois and Thomas Mann were convinced that it is "eccentrics" who make the world go round.

Though psychoanalytic diagnoses must be regarded with great caution, a remark by biographer Phyllis Greenacre may be apropos: Lewis Carroll's "Oedipal love for his mother was never displaced, except in typical Carroll fashion—by reversal—in which he incessantly fell in love with little girls."[6] Marquis de Sade, a man with strong sexual desires, had difficulty coming to orgasm. He devised many pain-inflicting forms of sexual activity. He also evolved an elaborate philosophy, based on his distinctive personal needs. So did every philosopher who ever lived—catering to his or her own unique personality—Epicurus and Spinoza and Schopenhauer and everyone else.

Erik Erikson traces the Protestant Reformation to Martin Luther's resolution of what Erikson calls "Life Stage: Identity and Role Confusion." According to psychiatrist Philip

Wessman, when John Wilkes Booth assassinated Lincoln, his rage was really directed against his father (in a basic Oedipal conflict) and against his envied older brother, actor Edwin Booth, who had been praised by Lincoln. Another psychiatrist attributes Lincoln's melancholia to a mother-fixation, reinforced by her early death. And still another biographer blames the outpourings of sexuality in Walt Whitman's poetry on his excessive attachment to his mother.

It is no coincidence that at one time almost 40% of the individuals who became psychiatric practitioners, in one form or another, exhibited symptoms of neurosis in youth. Reviewing Jung's *Analytical Psychology* Charles Rycroft observes: "Both Freud and Jung seem to have built into their theories and writings a conception and an interpretation of their own personalities."[7] Freud had a strong sex drive and assumed that the desire for sex was dominant in everyone. But recent studies in the United States indicate that approximately 20% of maladjusted individuals have no interest in sex.

Our own contemporaries seem no more capable of avoiding the rationalizing that emotional disturbance elicits. Poet Robert Lowell described his own manic-depression as "some flaw in the motor." In her study of the relationship between creative genius and emotional problems, psychologist Kay Jamison lists, among famous manic-depressives, composers Handel, Berlioz and Robert Schumann; poets Rossetti, Cowper, and Chatterton; writers Eugene O'Neill, Virgiana Woolf, John Ruskin, Hemingway, Scott Fitzgerald, and Charles Lamb. (As a result of a nervous breakdown, Lamb spent six weeks "very agreeably at a mad house at Hoxton.") Other writers whom Dr. Jamison considers manic-depressives are Byron, Shelley, Coleridge, Poe, and Gerard Manley Hopkins. Also American poets Hart Crane, Theodore Roethke, Delmore Schwartz, John Berryman, Anne Sexton, and Sylvia Plath.[8] This is not to say that all creative artists are manic-depressives. But the ones who suffer from this disorder reflect their condition in their art.

At different times Nietzsche offered different diagnoses of the world's problems. "All prejudices," he wrote in *Ecce Homo*, "may be traced back to the intestines. A sedentary life is the real sin against the Holy Ghost." And: "Unconscious gratitude for a good digestion (sometimes called ' brotherly love')."[9] Nietzsche, by the way, suffered from stomach ailments.

Nietzsche's Superman is an appropriate role model for Nietzsche—and perhaps for other psychotics who share his problems. But that Superman is not suitable for other people. The benevolence of Jesus is appropriate for Jesus— it is not achievable by most members of the hu-

man race. Every person must construct or select his or her own myth—and most people
choose, from among the available illusions, the
myths most suitable for their temperaments.

This certainly does not mean that all people
who seem to be happy are pretending. But it is
revealing to hear what Edith Sitwell said, at the
formal celebration of her 75th birthday: "I have
been very fortunate in my friends, have loved
them and been loved by them. . . . But if you
asked me if I have had a happy life, I must say
no—I have had an extremely unhappy life."

In a lengthy analysis of melancholy, Harold
Nicolson, Dame Sitwell's contemporary, tries to
find the causes of apparently "causeless melancholy." First he lists some obvious sources of
depression such as:

> unhappy childhood, unsuccessful love af-
> fairs, a nagging wife, an ill-tempered hus-
> band, uncongenial employment, persistent
> failure, acute poverty, denial of opportunity,
> . . . the injustice or malice of mankind . . .
> internal misfortunes [such as] ambition in
> excess of will power or capacity, extreme
> personal ugliness, an envious or jealous dis-
> position, self-pity, religious doubt, or a
> more than average lack of physical or moral
> courage.[10]

The most frequent causes of melancholy,
Nicolson concludes, are physical. Most of the
malcontents whom Nicolson studied are

> cursed either with some deformity that

hampers biological fulfillment, or with some functional weakness that prevents the easy elimination of waste products. Sainte-Beuve and Rousseau . . . suffered from hypospadias; Lucretius seemed to have been impotent; Beaudelaire, Nietzsche, Verlaine, and Byron were all afflicted with underdevelopment or sickness of the pituitary.[11]

Almost all American Nobel Prize winners in literature were alcoholics. Brendan Gill observes, in *Here at The New Yorker*, that almost every important modern American writer was a heavy drinker, listing "Faulkner, Hemingway, Fitzgerald, Lardner, Marquand, Sinclair Lewis, O'Hara, Hart Crane, E.A. Robinson, Wallace Stevens, O'Neill, Philip Barry, Edna St. Vincent Millay, Dorothy Parker, Hammett, Roethke, Benchley, and Berryman."[12]

Mary McCarthy traces literary genius to a very different source.

It cannot have been an accident . . . that so many of the best writers of this century have been consumptive: Lawrence, Kafka, Silone, Simone Weil, Camus, also Thomas Mann and Katherine Mansfield. . . . It may be significant that no American writer, so far as I know, has contracted tuberculosis, and no American writer of this age has been an inspired "voice," like Camus, like Orwell.[13]

Keats and Thoreau also were consumptives; one may speculate on the relationship between their writing and their feverish state.

Diagnoses of individuals who have concocted a world-view out of their own personal
problems are, of course, oversimplified. These
revelations may be amusing to us, and they
sometimes seemed amusing to the victims
themselves. Robert Burton, who spent his life
writing *Anatomy of Melancholy,* was portrayed
by Anthony Wood as "a melancholy and humorous person."[14] In his book Burton went so far as
to state: "This melancholy extends itself not to
men only, but even to vegetables." But Burton
was honest enough to admit: "If any man shall
ask, who am I that so boldly censures others,
have I no faults? Yes, more than thou hast, whoever thou art. I confess it again, I am as foolish,
as mad, as anyone."[15]

In every age contrasting beliefs exist, and
contemporaries disagree. At approximately the
same time Rousseau and De Sade evolved opposing philosophies: Man is naturally good vs.
Man is naturally vicious. It seems reasonable to
suspect that both Rousseau and De Sade concocted metaphysical systems to support the
spontaneous predilections that Rousseau and
De Sade already had. Like everyone else, these
two eighteenth-century Frenchmen were rationalizing.

Gamaliel Bradford, having written several
biographies of famous Americans, advised a
young writer, "Never begin a biography with

the statement 'So-and-so was a contradiction.' Everyone is." Some of these contradictions are hypocritical. For instance, Jean Jacques Rousseau, that apostle of humanitarianism, admits in his *Confessions:* "My five children were taken to the foundling hospital." And Somerset Maugham, admired for his sympathetic understanding of human nature, wrote at the end of a very long literary career, "I've always been interested in people, but I've never liked them."

It is an ironic fact that many people who cannot get along with their own families have the impudence to tell the world how it should rearrange itself for happier existence. One obvious explanation: it is precisely because these individuals feel guilty over their failure to get along with those close to them that they devise plans for utopian societies. People who could not alter the behavior of their neighbors try to reform entire nations. Men who have proved unable to change the deportment of their wives provide schemes for improving the conduct of whole cultures. Almost everyone wants to be liked; it is not a new suggestion that the idealistic plans of maladjusted reformers may be unconscious attempts to compensate for their own shortcomings. From Socrates to Karl Marx, hypocritical saviors have made "society's improvement" redemption for personal guilt.

This droll anomaly has not gone unobserved. Anatole France remarked: "Those who have given themselves the most concern about the happiness of peoples have made their neighbors very miserable." Bertrand Russell's daughter, Dr. Katherine Tait, wrote that he advocated women's suffrage but was a male chauvinist in his own private life. He behaved condescendingly toward women and expected his four wives—in proper sequence—to be subservient.

Many famous men, whose ideas and actions had momentous effect on history, did not themselves practice what they preached, nor do the things they did for the reasons they pretended to do them. It is easy to ignore the marital problems of Socrates, or the romantic failures of Nietzsche, or the bisexuality of Walt Whitman. Scholars superciliously brush away these facts as minor issues. But these are not irrelevant details. They are significant clues to temperamental characteristics that, far more than logical reasoning, account for the philosophies and conduct of human beings.

Karl Marx did not get along with his own family and showed his ineptitude in economics; after spending much of his life waiting for an inheritance, Marx lost it all on the London stock exchange. Lines from A. E. Houston's poems are often quoted as compassionate observations of human sorrow. But his brother Laurence revealed, after A. E.'s death, that the latter "kept a little notebook in which he jotted down hurtful and disparaging phrases as they occurred to him. He applied these phrases later when suitable enemies presented themselves."[16]

In his book on zen and motorcycles, Persig comments on the rigidity of the neo-Aristotleans at the University of Chicago, such as Hutchins and Adler and Crane, and their hostility to all opposing points of view. The immense knowledge of these men had no carryover at all to their behavior, personality, or temper. And that eminent leader of benevolent movements, Linus Pauling, admits that he was a negligent father who "didn't pay much attention to the children."

Arthur Sullivan was a frustrated writer of serious music who despised the melodies he had to create for Gilbert's operettas. Don Marquis became famous for poems about Archy the Cockroach while he labored to produce a profound religious poem. And Aldous Huxley never let his mysticism interfere with his enjoyment of sybaritic living.

When Sartre's *Autobiography* was published, several reviewers observed that the basic elements of modern Existentialism stem from the severe problems Sartre had as a child. (But the same reviewers did not concede that their own philosophies stemmed from their own childhood experiences and genetic heritages.)

It is no secret that most great humorists were profoundly discontented human beings, the misery of Dorothy Parker simply proving that the unhappiness of great wits is not limited to males. Samuel Johnson is another sage whose philosophy was an expression of his own peculiar temperament rather than a balanced worldview. Boswell tells us that Johnson said "he never had a moment in which death was not terrible to him." Attempting to explain Johnson's pessimism, Boswell blames heredity. Johnson's father, he says, had "that disease, the nature of which eludes the most minute enquiry, though the effects are well known to be a weariness of life . . . and a general sensation of gloomy wretchedness. From him then his son inherited with some other qualities, 'a vile melancholy,' which in his too strong expression of any disturbance of the mind, 'made him mad all his life, at least not sober." Johnson told Boswell: "Alas! It is all outside; I may be cracking my joke, and cursing the sun."[17]

Reviewing *The Passion of Ayn Rand*, Carlin Romano wrote: "She lacked any philosophical competence—a pronounced flaw in someone who called for the 'supremacy of reason.'. . . She interprets every philosophical doctrine opposed to hers as a 'rationalization for psychological weakness.'" (There is an amusing element in Alice Rosenbaum's choice of her American name: "She took 'Ayn' from a Finnish writer she'd never read and 'Rand' from the typewriter she had with her.")[18]

Tchaikovsky is another artist the contradictions of whose life are ironic at best, hypocritical at worst. Analyzing Tchaikovsky's achievements, Dale Harris wrote: "Like most creators, Tchaikovsky could express in his work a comprehensive and mature view of human nature that he was incapable of in his daily life." The Russians have made Tchaikovsky a national treasure, an artist of the people, a cultural hero. But in a letter to his benefactress he wrote: "I work for myself alone and care only for myself." And, Dale Harris concludes, Tchaikovsky was "politically reactionary and morally corrupt. . . . Far from sympathizing with the oppressed, he was an upholder of czarist autocracy. . . . He was pathologically unstable, profoundly pessimistic, and a homosexual."[19]

The contradictions of great philosophers were clearly apparent to Robert Burton. "Socrates, 'the wisest man then living,'. . . was an illiterate idiot, as Aristophanes called him, *irrisor et ambitiousus,* as Aristotle terms him, an enemy of all arts and sciences, an opionative ass, a caviller, a kind of pedant; for his manners, as Theod. Cyrensis describes him, a Sodomite, an atheist, a pot-companion, by Plato's own confession, a sturdy drinker. . . . Pythagoras was part philosopher, part magician, or part witch. . . . Their actions, opinions in general were so prodigious, absurd, ridiculous, their books and elaborate treatises were full of dotage . . . their lives being opposite to their words, they commended poverty to others, and were most covetous themselves, extolled love and peace, and yet persecuted one another with virulent hate and malice. They could give precepts for verse and prose, but not a man of them could moderate his affections."[20]

One may make what one will out of James Harvey Robinson's description of Aristotle: "He was reported to have had very thin legs and small eyes, and he was wont to indulge in very conspicuous rings and was accustomed to arrange his hair carefully."[21]

If philosophers create philosophies to satisfy their own needs, it seems reasonable to suppose that the founders of the world's religions also fashioned systems of theology that fit their own temperaments. And within every major religion the worshippers tend to fall into three categories: the fundamentalists, who believe literally and fervently; the majority, who believe conveniently, accepting some and ignoring much of their religion's dicta; and the liberals, who accept the spirit but not the letter of each theology.

Philosophers have always sought the truth, the nature of reality. But the list of philosophies that great thinkers have expressed and lesser minds have accepted is very long; it is hard to believe that only one of them is the correct explanation. The list includes idealism, transcendentalism; phenomenalism, realism, nominalism, positivism, logical positivism; existentialism, voluntarism; holism; rationalism, humanism, hedonism; utilitarianism, materialism; pragmatism; relativism; agnosticism, skepticism, Pyrrhonism; eclecticism; fatalism; Pythagoreanism, Platonism, Aristotleanism, Stoicism, Epicureanism, Cynicism; Neoplatonism; gnosticism; scholasticism, Thomism; Cartesianism, Berkeleyanism, Kantianism; Hegelianism, dialectical materialism, Marxism; Bergsonism; yoga, Vedanta; and monism, pluralism.

Throughout history eminent scholars have expressed totally conflicting conclusions. They were all intelligent individuals who looked at the same evidence and reached contradictory opinions about the meaning of that evidence. These scholars were not, and are not, necessarily dishonest or corrupt. They were, in free societies, interpreting data as their temperaments and experience forced them to interpret data.

Even though all philosophies are rationalizations, they are still valuable. The aggregate of individual rationales is a useful summary of the beliefs existing in the world. Individuals who dislike conflict and competition devise—usually unconsciously—concepts like socialism and utopia. Persons who relish competition and conflict devise—usually unconsciously—concepts like capitalism and social Darwinism. None of these concepts works perfectly; every society contains human beings of opposing temperaments. Calvin and Freud considered the anti-social elements in human personality to be predominant. But Jesus and psychiatrists like Karen Horney and Harry Stack Sullivan taught that "doing good" and "helping" are healthy impulses, not necessarily compensations for guilty feelings.

Throughout history philosophers have made the same mistake that most people make: because they had a piece of the truth they assumed they had the whole truth; and because they had a truth they assumed it was the only truth.

Six

Environmental

He who does not lie never grows up.
—Proverb of Gaude tribe, Africa

Freud once said, "Civilization is repression." He was referring not to the coercion of govern- ment but the constraints imposed by society on the members of a civilized community. In order to function smoothly, every society evolves an elaborate assortment of customs, traditions, and behavior patterns that the members of that so- ciety are expected to accept and practice. Pow- erful social forces discourage deviation from conformist behavior. Henri Bergson suggested that humor was society's method of ridiculing nonconformists in order to make them comply with the group's behavior patterns. But individuals are all different, and in their own discrete ways they fail to conform. Then they try to conceal some of these failures by hypocritical actions and remarks.

As human beings evolved from the level of open conflict in primitive society to the camouflaged competition of "civilization," they learned to repress their spontaneous reactions and to reveal them only in socially approved form. In the early stages of human existence competition for food, sex, and survival was clearly apparent. Everyone knew that he or she was contending with others, and that the penalty for defeat was hunger or frustration or death. In civilized society the competition is concealed under a veneer of superficial courtesy. But everyone is still competing with everyone else for food, sex, survival, and a higher place in his or her hierarchy.

In all human society, and in every sub-section of society, there is a pecking order. In some cultures this hierarchical element is openly admitted; in other cultures the pretense is made, especially by underlings, that everyone is equal. But from chickens and cows to soldiers and professors, everyone has a place in the hierarchy. An old African proverb says, "Even the fingers on one's hand are not equal." Only successful aggression, or chance, alters one's place in the hierarchy. The difference between "primitive" and "civilized" society is that in the latter there is an unwritten agreement to pretend that competition is not a permanent condition of life. A sugarcoating of politeness spreads a veneer over the unremitting contention underneath. In this environment of camouflaged competition and shifting hierarchies, hypocrisy is inevitable.

As societies become more and more civilized, individuals become more and more dependent upon each other and upon the state. In the eighteenth century, four out of five Americans were self-employed; in 1985 only one out of five worked for himself or herself. People who are dependent on others for their livelihood learn very quickly that they have to control their spontaneous expressions of opinion and emotion. One's superiors do not like to be criticized or opposed or mocked. The person who moves most rapidly up the hierarchical ladder "adapts" and dissimulates and maneuvers; he or she justifies the hypocritical behavior by describing it as pragmatic or tactful or necessary.

In a "developed" society hypocrisy is indispensable. As anthropologist Robin Fox observes, young males learn what kind of behavior is required in a "compromise" society, restrain their natural aggression, and develop such characteristics as being "controlled" and "cunning." Near the end of the twentieth century, more cultures than ever before claimed to be "civilized."

Almost nothing that a human being says constitutes the whole truth. A statement by an individual or an institution may contain a tiny portion of the truth, or a large part of the truth, or the complete antithesis of the truth. But it rarely comprises the entire truth.

It is not hard to understand why almost every statement made by a human being concerning his or her interaction with another human being must be accepted as only partially true. Descriptions of the same event by persons involved in it will differ. Usually the reason for the difference is not deliberate lying or calculated misrepresentation. Every person experiences every event from one's own perspective, in terms of one's own momentary condition, under the pressures of one's own desires and fears. When two children scream to their parents an account of their squabble, two different narratives are presented. When two witnesses give their evidence, disparities are immediately apparent. When two experts testify in court they offer conflicting reports. An extraterrestrial visitor to Earth would do well not to accept as objective truth the statement of any human being, no matter how sincere or charming the Earthling is. The truth is not in him or her.

Hypocrisy exists among "primitive" people, and it is flagrantly on display in highly developed societies. It is not an exaggeration to say that the more civilized a nation is, the more hypocritical it is. That is so because "civilized" communities set up such high standards of behavior, such admirable objectives, that most human beings cannot meet the desired requirements. But most human beings in civilized society feel guilty about their failure to practice the ideals of their society and try to disguise the motivations for their behavior.

Several years ago a sociologist at an American university proposed an experiment when the class was studying "honesty." He suggested that for one entire day the students be totally honest in all their relationships. After a half day of speaking nothing but the truth, a female student was reported by her roommate to the psychiatrist at the University Health Center. The roommate thought that the sociology student was having a nervous breakdown. Life without dissimulation is impossible in what we call civilized society. The question is not whether everyone is a hypocrite. Everyone is. The only variant is the degree of hypocrisy practiced by every person.

T. S. Eliot described the social process as "prepare a face to meet a face." Ann Morrow Lindbergh felt that the necessity for constant posturing was the most uncomfortable aspect of social existence. In *Gift from the Sea* she wrote: "The most exhausting thing in life, I have discovered, is being insincere. That is why so much social life is exhausting; one is wearing a mask." Eugene O'Neill, in *Great God Brown,* makes his characters wear masks when they engage in social intercourse—and sometimes even when they are alone. We cannot dispense with posing; all we can do is change images, by choice or therapy or plastic surgery. As one wit put it, "No pose is also a pose."

Apparently there is enough lying going on constantly in our society to justify a contest. *The Des Moines Register* sponsored a "Lies, Lies, Nothing But Lies" competition in which entrants were asked to consider the following questions: What is the lie most often told in our society? Do you have a favorite lie? Do you have a most congenial lie? And a recent survey by psychologists showed that the average university student lies at least twice a day and uses "white lies" much more often.

When George Santayana remarked that the world is a perpetual mockery of what it pretends to be, he was describing a very old phenomenon. There is nothing new about organized hypocrisy. Claques have been hired for centuries to applaud entertainers and political candidates or to show public disapproval of singers and cam-

paigners. In India there have always been professional mourners available for participation
in funerals at which they express loud and violent grief for deceased individuals whom they
do not know. In ancient Greece certain men con-
gregated near judicial buildings, indicating by
the straw in their shoes that they were available as witnesses, pro or con, for any plaintiff
or defendant who was willing to pay for false
evidence.

Sociologist Erving Goffman's metaphor for
human behavior in public is that of an actor on
stage. It consists of the performance of many
and frequently changing roles in the presence
of others. In a social situation, Goffman says,
every individual "intentionally conveys misin-
formation" about himself by two types of communication: he gives misleading information
and he gives off false information (that is, he
feigns). Goffman cites as an example the girl in
a university dormitory who will "allow herself
to be called several times, in order to give all
the other girls ample opportunity to hear her
paged."[1]

Sociobiologist Edward Wilson agrees with
Goffman. Men and women have expanded their
social activities "into great networks where individuals consciously alter roles from hour to
hour as if changing masks. . . . Each occupation—the physician, the judge, the waiter—is

played just so," says Wilson, "regardless of the true workings of the mind behind the persona.... The actor continually reassesses his persona and the impact his behavior is having on others."[2]

The amount of repression that society requires in different situations varies enormously, but for the average person there is not much interaction with other people that permits completely honest expression.

Because there is so much hypocrisy constantly on display in everyday life, there develops for all but the most naive members of society an "expectation of hypocrisy." We learn not to take literally casual inquiries about our health or to take seriously superficial expressions of good will like "Have a nice day." Because there is so much pretense in everyday civilized behavior, we get accustomed to that pretense and we expect it.

If Goffman and Wilson are right—and one can disagree with them only on the *extent* of role-playing that exists in society—the necessity for hypocritical behavior is inescapable. One can't leave home without it.

. . . .

Because "civilized" society requires a great deal of pretense, an honest statement can, under certain conditions, be amusing. It is not truth itself that is humorous; it is only truth at a socially inappropriate or embarrassing moment that is humorous. When the hypocrisy of society makes us expect an *untruthful* remark, the honest statement strikes us as a surprise. We realize immediately that the surprise is pleasant because we enjoy the violation of an artificial restriction.

Much of the "humor" of children's remarks consists simply of naïve honesty at inopportune moment, such as the comments of Dennis the Menace or of the characters in Schulz's *Peanuts*. The clown, fool, and court jester use this stratagem, being permitted (as "abnormal" members of society) to express inconvenient truths instead of the expected lies. Freud identified this species of comic technique as the *naïve*. It appears, wrote Freud, when someone "puts himself completely outside of inhibition, because it does not exist for him." The naïve one presumably has no intention of making us laugh; he or she is certain (or pretends to be certain) that the remarks and actions are quite proper. But the audience that is listening to these remarks, or watching these actions, has inhibitions, and knows that it has them.

In Bernard Shaw's *Devil's Disciple* three very different characters achieve humor by expressing unexpected truth at three different levels. The brother, a fool, is permitted to tell the truth because he is *below* society; Dick Dudgeon, the devil's disciple, can tell the truth because he is *outside* of society; and General Burgoyne nonchalantly tells the truth because he is *above* society.

A great many hypocritical pretenses are immediately exposed by an unexpectedly truthful remark. Louis MacNeice wrote, "Being a poet, I am prejudiced against the novel; because novels are so many and, comparatively, so easy to read, they interfere with my market." Heinrich Heine said it was easy to account for his motive in criticizing Goethe: "It was envy." And a psychiatrist who specializes in family relations admitted: "When my wife said to me, 'Your teen-aged daughter just called me a bitch. What are you going to do about it?' I told her, 'I'm going into the bathroom and lock the door.'"

Ichiro Kawasaki, Japan's Ambassador to Argentina in 1969, forgot the cardinal rule of politics when he published a book called *Japan Unmasked*. In it he wrote: "The immaturity of the Japanese is particularly noticeable in the realm of diplomacy." Also: "Japanese politicians, once elected, are given a free hand to consolidate their positions to their advantage with a mixture of bribes and threats, openly backed by administrative power." And the cruelest cut of all: "Of all the races of the world, the Japanese are physically perhaps the least attractive, with exception of pygmies and Hottentots." Ambassador Kawasaki was immediately asked for his resignation by the Foreign Minister of Japan.

A simple statement of unexpected truth can reveal hypocrisy more convincingly than hours of argument. Campaigning for women's rights, Florence Kennedy said, "If men could get pregnant, abortion would be a sacrament." A licensed fur trapper, Ken Bates, told a crusader against hunting, "The only people with a right to complain about what I do for a living are vegetarian nudists." Politician Andrew Young observed, "Nothing is illegal if a hundred businessmen do it." And an eminent churchman, Dean Inge, admitted at the age of 93: "I still know nothing about the three most important questions: Eternity, Human Personality, and Evil."

When John Kendrick Bangs had run for mayor and been defeated, he was asked by a reporter for *The New York Times*, "To what do you attribute your defeat?" "Too few votes," said Bangs. In Shaw's *Devil's Disciple*, Major Swindon asks indignantly, "What will History say?" General Burgoyne replies: "History will tell lies as usual." And a Bill Mauldin cartoon shows President De Gaulle saying, "Why do you Americans stay where you are not wanted?" Behind De Gaulle is a French cemetery filled with American graves.

Unexpected truth sometimes startles us out of platitudinous attitudes. Lin Yutang, for example, wrote, "We seldom realize that the rise of the Peripatetic School of Greek philosophy was due to Madam Socrates. If Socrates were in the soft arms of a loving wife and remained in his house, he would not be going about the streets of Athens and collaring wayfarers and asking them awkward question." And W.H. Auden admitted how little influence artists have. "Political social history would be no different if Dante, Michelangelo, Byron had never lived. Nothing I wrote against Hitler prevented one Jew from being killed. In the end, art is small beer."

Hegel admitted: "Peoples and governments have never learned anything from history, or acted on principles deduced from it." A few years ago, an American sociologist returning from a government-sponsored visit to a developing country in Africa, said: "It is useless to teach these people about proper nutrition. Their problem is simple survival." And the Indian poet Tagore wrote, "I do not love him because he is good, but because he is my little boy."

Two Japanese *senryu* are relevant here:

Even Buddha
Cannot save
Those without money.

When we give back
What we have borrowed
We feel as if we have been robbed.
(Sankasushi)

All over the world, proverbs express uncomfortable truths. The Japanese say: "While on a journey, one need not feel shame" and "Telling a lie is sometimes expedient." Also: "Praying to God only when in distress." Another *senryu* tells us:

> The parasite;
> What he says in his sleep
> Is the truth.

In several Chinese proverbs the use of unexpected truth results in humor at the expense of hypocrisy. As in the following:

> A man who has a beautiful soul always has some beautiful things to say but a man who says beautiful things does not necessarily have a beautiful Soul.
> (Confucius)

> If good luck comes, who doesn't? If good luck does not come, who does?

> When beating a dog, first find out who his owner is.

Before Sammy Davis, Jr. married a Jewish wife, he studied with a rabbi who prepared him for conversion to Judaism. Afterwards, a joke about the episode made the rounds. In this version, Davis offers the rabbi one expensive gift after another to express his gratitude. The rabbi refuses all of them. Davis insists, and the rabbi finally says, "If you really want to do something for me, Sammy, don't buy a house in my neighborhood." The story is not true, but the social criticism is accurate.

Honest comments by foreign visitors are sometimes amusing. Robert Burton wrote, "A

68

Sybarite of old, supping in Sparta and observing their hard fare, said it was no marvel if the Laecedomonians were valiant men; 'for his part he would rather run upon a sword point (and so would any man in his wits) than live with such base diet, or lead so wretched a life."[3]

The modern Yugoslavian satirist, Branco Crncevic, includes among his aphorisms: "Speak honestly and quietly, the more honestly, the more quietly." Cato said about his fellow Romans: "We govern all the world abroad, and our wives at home rule us." When Boswell remarked that there was much criticism of Samuel Johnson's accepting a pension from King George III, Johnson replied: "I wish my pension were twice as large, that they make twice as much noise."[4]

A cartoon caption by the modern humorist Guidon says: "The good Lord never gives you more than you can handle. Unless you die of something." Mencken wrote: "The meek shall inherit the earth—and the strong will take it away from them." And in ancient Greece, Anaxagoras told a man who was grieving because he was dying in a foreign land, "The descent to Hades is the same from every place."

Again and again, the simple statement of unexpected truth pleases us by exposing hypocrisy. In a play he wrote two thousand years ago, Terence made a character say, "Rigorous law is often rigorous injustice." Goethe observed, "When ideas fail, words come in very handy." The so-called cynicism of La Rochefoucauld is often nothing but the expression of truth: "We always like those who admire us." When asked what was the proper time for dinner, Diogenes replied, "If you are rich, whenever you please; if you are poor, whenever you can." Ogden Nash remarked, "Progress might have been all right once but it has gone on too long."

When we hear the truth expressed unexpectedly in a society that has accustomed itself to expect hypocrisy, we are pleased because we are enjoying the violation of an artificial social restriction. Everywhere in the world this is understood, as in the ancient Indian proverb "No one wants to hear an unpleasant truth." In Ceylon (Sri Lanka) the proverb says: "The truthful man finds no room even in the tavern." And among the Gaude tribesmen of Africa there is a proverb: "He who does not lie never grows up."

Seven

Administration

*The only thing an administrator should be
concerned with is what works.*

Sinclair Lewis described administrators as
"men of measured merriment." The Peter Principle applies to them: administrators rise to their
level of incompetence. And Parkinson's Law
fits: the work expands in proportion to the authority the executive can generate. If successful administrators are hypocritical and ruthless,
it may be because hypocrisy and ruthlessness
are indispensable characteristics of administrative success. To the detached observer, the ability of administrators to restrain expressions of
approval or criticism—in order to avoid possible
future complications—is amusing. But this continuous weighing of possible implications kills

all spontaneity. It may make a successful political creature; it certainly makes an artificial human being.

The decision-making of administrators has nothing to do with abstract justice. A chief executive officer, later president of the company, lectured to his administrative colleagues: "I hear too much talk about right and wrong; the only thing an administrator should be concerned with is what works." In situations that are not routine, decisions of administrators are influenced by the places of the antagonists in the hierarchy, the personal relationship between the top administrator and the competitors, and the probable effect of the decision on the smooth operation of the bureaucracy.

As administrators, good persons often make evil decisions because the bureaucratic system requires them to do so. It is not just that conventional ethics are irrelevant to management; ethics often interfere with smooth administrative procedure. Ethics not only don't belong, they are often inimical to efficient conduct of affairs.

In administration, as in many other aspects of civilized living, form tends to transcend content. Lin Yutang wrote that Chinese humor "consists in complying with outward form and total disregard of the substance." Chinese humor is not unique in this respect. As long as "correct procedure" is followed, the bureaucracy approves, no matter how heinous the results. As long as the established procedure is conformed to, administrators defend the actions of other bureaucrats, even when those actions were motivated by spite, malice, revenge, petty jealousy, or sheer stupidity.

It is human nature to approve what pleases us and to oppose what we don't like, regardless of objective evidence. Administrators share this prejudice. Many scientists have learned that when their research disproves the conclusions that a bureaucracy favors, they will lose support for that research. Dr. Irwin Bross was not alone when he claimed that the National Cancer Institute failed to renew his grant because his findings went against official Federal policy on radiation and nuclear energy. Dr. Karl Morgan, former director of health physics at the Oak Ridge National Laboratory, agreed: "My belief is that the findings [of Dr. Bross] were contrary to the wishes of the agencies supporting these programs." Bernard Frank, an expert in statistics, resigned his administrative position in the Federal government because the results of statistical studies were continually twisted by top administrators to support the views of the administration or to contradict the statements of the opposition. Mark Twain was right when he said, "Figures don't lie, but liars figure."

Eight

Higher Education

Groups of fishes, lizards, various birds, and many mammals including man are often organized into social hierarchies.
W. C. Allee

Woodrow Wilson had been president of Princeton University before he became President of the United States. He told a professional politician that the politics of university administration were more vicious than those of government. It may be, as Professor Thomas Friedman suggests, that the arguments in university politics are so bitter because the issues are so unimportant. The maneuvers, conflicts, and betrayals are more politely executed in the pseudo-serenity of the university environment, but the results are as brutal and unjust as they are in a Chicago precinct. An English professor who writes excellent detective novels, Robert Barnard, described a character in these words: "There was in his manner a nervous intensity that contained the odd mixture of aggression and defensiveness that rodents have, and those who engage in university politics."[1]

If rationalizing is a common characteristic, university administrators are a perfect illustration. Top-level officials demonstrate, logically, politely, and unblushingly, that black is white and wrong is right. And, on later occasions, they insist, logically, politely, and unblushingly, that black is not white and right is not wrong. Since most people are inconsistent it is not surprising that administrators contradict themselves. What is disturbing is the panache with which they lie, the sanctimoniousness with which they misrepresent, the nonchalance with which they pervert reality. University administrators are especially articulate priests of hypocrisy.

Scholarly ability has nothing to do with a university administrator's qualifications. Giovanni Batista Vico (1668-1744), one of Italy's greatest historians, spent four years preparing himself by intensive study for a prestigious professorship. But he neglected to cultivate the necessary political connections. The result: his two unqualified opponents received fifteen and fourteen votes each; Vico received none. That

Vico is still famous, while his successful antagonists have been long forgotten, is evidence that
in Italy too the law of success says: Hypocrisy:
Don't leave home without it.

In every organization, administrators are
arranged in a hierarchy, a pecking order similar
to that of animals. As W. C. Allee put it:

> Groups of fishes, lizards, various birds, and
> many mammals including man are often or-
> ganized into social hierarchies. The social
> order usually rests on threats or on the di-
> rect use of force. . . . High position in the
> peck order gives more ready access to food,
> space, mates, and to other things that are
> important to hens.[2]

Although universities pretend to be democratic institutions, the hierarchical structure rivals that of the military. The president is responsible to a board of trustees or governors, and
there are enough vice-presidents to satisfy
Parkinson's Law. Deans proliferate, as do associate deans and assistant deans. Then come department heads and department chairpersons
and assistant heads and assistant chairpersons.
There are also endowed professors and Distinguished Professors and ordinary professors and
associate professors and assistant professors and
instructors and assistants. There are instructors
on tenure track and instructors on non-tenure
track. There are adjunct (meaning "temporary")
appointments at every level.

In theory, everyone is equal. In fact, everyone with tenure is a citizen and everyone without tenure is an alien. And although tenured citizens are equal, some are much more equal than others. Education is only one of the activities of a modern university, not necessarily the primary one. There is research, there is the continual pursuit of grants, there is incessant contacting of individuals for contributions. And, in many universities, there are athletics and the continued demands of alumni and local newspapers for successful athletic teams—and indignant exposés by the same newspapers of illegitimate activity in getting and keeping outstanding athletes.

In a university, administrators are commercial functionaries in an educational enterprise. Often, they had decided that, since mediocre administrators are paid twice as much as mediocre professors, they might as well be doubly rewarded for their mediocrity.

To compensate for their intellectual deficiencies university administrators persuade themselves that their contribution to the university is far more important than that of scholars and teachers. It is their skills, they insist, that keep a university functioning smoothly. It is their foresight, they claim, that anticipates change and prepares for it. Like the non-university administrator, the academic bureaucrat proceeds on the assumption that justice is irrelevant, morality is inapplicable, and loyalty is inconvenient.

Jealous of the scholars over whom they have putative authority, typical university administrators harass them in ways that they consider safe, though they try to avoid direct confrontations or open expression of hostility. They pretend that every one of their actions is motivated by the long-range good of the university. Never, never are they expressing personal animosity or engaging in a vendetta or indulging in revenge. Often nonentities themselves, they sanctimoniously nag at genuine scholars and superior teachers.

Being an administrator often changes people drastically. The administration buildings of American universities contain many people who were once decent, tolerant, and open-minded human beings. Now they are secretive, non-committal, cautious, and calculating. No longer is spontaneity permitted. If they had a reputation for idealism before they became administrators, they limit their idealism to words, never to actions. They become apologists for the administration. Or they remain progressive on international issues and on abstract concepts, but 100% supportive of the local administration in specific instances, regardless of how repressive or reactionary the local administration proves to be.

For some inhabitants of academia, service on committees becomes a useful step on the journey to administration. As committee members, many educators begin to give up their independence of judgment and their personal criteria. Instead they learn to rely more and more on tradition, "rules," and the hints dropped by the committee chairperson about the wishes of higher authority.

The metamorphosis from person-as-committee-member to person-as-administrator is easily achieved. Having already subordinated private ethics to the institution's needs, the new administrator rationalizes away all other conflicts between ordinary human decency and bureaucratic efficiency, between compassion and whatever "bottom line" the organization requires. Evolution did not stop with the human being. It went onward—or backward—to create two new species: Man-as-administrator and Woman as-administrator.

Absurdities abound among administrators. A dean of engineering at one school used Dale Carnegie's *How to Win Friends* as a textbook in his class. When the University of Illinois built a football stadium in 1924, it made sure that there were 150 more seats than in the Wisconsin stadium. The graduation ceremonies at universities are anachronisms, including at Ivy League colleges the use of Latin by graduating students who don't know a word of Latin. (At a recent Princeton graduation ceremony, the seniors were given a sheet of instructions telling them when to applaud, cheer, and laugh during the Latin speech to which they were listening.)

When deans interview outstanding scholars whom they want to lure to their university, they routinely make promises that they know they will not be able to keep. They promise facilities, they promise equipment, they promise future financial arrangements. Woe to the naive scholar who believes anything that is not specifically and definitively written down. The spoken word of the administrator is often untrustworthy, whether it is spoken to other administrators or to ingenuous individuals. The administrator knows this and proceeds accordingly. The foolish non-administrator who thinks that the ordinary rules of honesty apply to the statements of administrators quickly and painfully learns otherwise.

Among the devices used by administrators is the following: department heads give one member of their staff large raises, then use these figures as leverage to get their own salaries raised above those of any professor in their department. The professors whom H. L. Mencken despised most were those in the liberal arts. A look at their salaries proves that administrators share Mencken's contempt.

When he was no longer chancellor of the California system of higher education, Clark Kerr wrote: "The three major problems on a campus are sex for the student, athletics for the alumni, and parking for the faculty."[3]

One time-honored absurdity is the overwhelming, incessant demand for faculty members to fill out forms. The forms are intended to measure time-use, attitudes, conditions, and a thousand other aspects of campus life. Nothing constructive is ever done about the information revealed by these questionnaires. They are sent through computers, thousands of copies are made, and they are all filed away somewhere for some hypothetical future use. Experienced faculty members soon lose patience with these questionnaires and fill them with imaginary or absurd data. And administrators, blissfully ignorant of the law for computers—"Garbage in, garbage out"—continue to quote the results of the questionnaires for whatever purposes exist at the moment. There is an Alice-in-Wonderland quality about the attempts of machines to identify qualities that differentiate inspirational educators from the administrators who make up the questionnaires.

Since many people desire some form of immortality, university presidents have devised a special means of stimulating, and controlling, their administrators. They name buildings after themselves, university streets after vice-presidents and deans, dormitory units after department heads, and miscellaneous locations and structures after prominent educators who have pleased the establishment. Abrasive brilliance is ignored; the Thorstein Veblens are not memorialized. So while deans go about jockeying for position and sending out to their colleges Xeroxed copies of their platitudinous speeches, they keep constantly in mind the prospect of having an alley, a path, a lane, perhaps a street named after them—and they consider, before making a controversial decision, what effect that decision will have on the eponymyzing process in the not-too-distant future.

In a remarkable number of instances, the ambitious administrator reaches the decision that his superiors would like to have him reach. Being a "team player" is one of the euphemisms that corporations, the American presidency, and university administrations use to describe this decision-making process.

In the sixteenth century a wise essayist, Michel Montaigne, wrote: "I have seen in my time a hundred artisans, a hundred plowmen, wiser and happier than rectors of the university, and whom I would rather resemble." The typical university president always says the right thing but always does the expedient thing, regardless of how contradictory his statement and his action are.

Lord Acton, a historian, is remembered for his aphorism: "Power corrupts—absolute power corrupts absolutely." For university presidents who have been in office a long time another maxim should be added: "Power brutalizes—absolute power brutalizes absolutely." Persons who were decent and sensitive human beings become, after lengthy terms as university presidents, urbane autocrats. They cultivate a smoothness. Unlike the Red Queen, who shouted "Off with their heads" whenever she was displeased, the seasoned university president coos, "I regret exceedingly the unavoidable necessity of removing your admirable head from the remainder of your worthy body."

Toward the end of their administration typical presidents have forgotten that members of the proletariat—that is, non-administrators—have feelings. Presidents are loyal to their staffs and support them without reservation in their conflicts with the faculty. Their allegiance to administrators transcends obligations to the faculty, minimizes respect for justice, and obliterates sensitivity to human emotions. They cherish to the end the delusion that they are loved by faculty and students.

It was administrators like that, ages ago, who provided the model for the three monkeys: see no evil, hear no evil, speak no evil. But, like those primates, the typical university president sees, hears, and speaks quickly on every issue that concerns his or her personal welfare.

In every occupation there are jokes about authority-figures. Exaggerated though they may be, the jokes reveal essential truths about the authorities and about the occupation. In one such jest, a young assistant professor returns from war service and is told by the president that, because of budgetary problems, his position has been eliminated. The professor is shocked. "Isn't there some other job on campus I can have?" "No, I'm sorry." "Can I be in charge of tutoring?" "No, I'm sorry." The professor gets angry and pounds the table. "Well, I'll be a son-of-a-bitch!" he shouts. "Why didn't you say so?" the president says. "In that case we'll make you a dean."

In another campus joke, the deans of American universities and their families are on a ship carrying them to a deans' convention. Fire breaks out and everyone has to jump into the water. Soon sharks appear and begin eating the women and children. A dean calls out to a passing shark who has ignored him, "Why are you leaving the deans alone?" The shark grins and replies, "Professional courtesy."

If Peter's Principle is sound, long-time department heads are likely to be more dissatisfied than other university administrators because they reach their level of incompetence at a lower stage than other executives. The failure to be promoted may embitter long-term department heads, but it never causes them to behave less sycophantically or less hypocritically than they had before.

Anthropologist Ashley Montagu may well have been right when he wrote, in the *American Way of Life*, "An administration as such is wholly unnecessary in a college or university, except, of course, for janitors, plumbers, and keepers of the grounds and buildings." It is a tribute to the cold-bloodedness and other reptilian qualities of academic executives that when psychologists Raymond Cattell and Ivan H. Scheier measured anxiety in American life they concluded, "Least anxious of all, on the Cattell-Scheier scale, are university administrators."

. . . .

At the university level, education seems even more hypocritical than it is because of the high standards that educators pretend to accept. The spokespeople for higher education utter noble platitudes, but their personal motivations remain as selfish as any other business person's and their objectives are as self-centered as those of any other opportunist. The public may think of professors as impartial, mature individuals, influenced only by external data and making rational decisions unrelated to prejudices and self-interest. To anyone who is familiar with university faculties, this notion is hilarious.

Professor Thomas Kuhn estimated that the acceptance of new ideas in science is delayed for anywhere from five to fifteen years in university communities. The reasons: a disinclination on the part of professors to admit that what they had been teaching is wrong; resentment against disturbers of academic conformity; jealousy; and sheer laziness. Now that scholars admit scientific knowledge becomes outdated in five years, the pace of acceptance has quickened. But the same psychological, and hypocritical, processes continue to function in the halls of academe.

Original ideas in the social sciences may take a century to penetrate the minds of professors. And a new and true concept in the arts still has to overcome the influence of Aristotle in the minds of modern academicians. Ideas in the arts cannot be demonstrated with the ostensible objectivity of evidence in the sciences. So, for the same reasons as in science, but with greater latitude for rejection, professors today ignore ideas that they did not learn when they were students. As with teachers of science, professors in the arts would have to admit that they were wrong, lazy, jealous of competitors, or resentful of challengers to the status quo.

The collective courage of university faculties, as far as protecting mistreated colleagues is concerned, fits into the proverbial thimble. And this in spite of the fact that most faculty members have tenure and cannot be dismissed from their jobs.

Faculties are timid on every issue—except in demands for higher salaries—and they support or oppose administrators for reasons that have nothing to do with the welfare of the school or of the students. Members of the faculty scramble for promotions, jockey for raises, and maneuver for grants. They indulge in petty jealousies, vicious revenges, and nasty vendettas. The same kinds of conflicts exist among highly educated human beings as among all others. The main difference is that the hypocrisy in academia is better concealed.

More faculty members belong to the American Association of University Professors than to any other professional organization. So it is revealing that when the AAUP at a large university arranges a meeting to discuss improved teaching techniques, fifteen or twenty people attend. But when the AAUP calls a meeting to discuss faculty salaries and retirement benefits, hundreds of educators turn up. Professors, like plumbers, want to get as much money as they can. The fact that the plumber's income is considerably higher than the average instructor's salary is simply a reflection of what society considers more important: a stuffed toilet or an open mind.

A typical gathering of university English teachers for coffee break begs for the comic playwright's pen. Everyone in the group is waiting to make a comment about his of her recent achievement—a book, an article, a speech, an award—and ignores all other subjects. No one pays attention to the topic of conversation; everyone is thinking of ways to maneuver the discussion around to his or her own agenda. There is subtly expressed jealousy over the promotion of one competing colleague and subtly expressed pleasure over the passing-over of another competing colleague. There is belittling of the published work of one colleague and sly ridicule of the failure of another to get published. One faction emphasizes the importance of technique; it is correct methodology that is all-important, they insist. Indignantly, another faction responds; no, no, it is the content that matters. Ad infinitum the prattle goes on. No one's mind is changed, no one learns anything, and no one says anything original or profound.

In a recent book, Professor Leroy Wolins of Iowa State University charged that a large amount of the published material in academic journals is based on defective or inadequate research, as far as the statistical elements are concerned. Not only are the data manipulated by the authors to obtain the results they are trying to get, but a considerable amount of hypocrisy permeates the process by which submitted papers are selected. Professor Wolins found that the old-boy network operates among the referees of scholarly journals and, when pseudonyms were used, the same papers received very different evaluations from the erudite, and presumably objective, referees.

The intelligentsia cannot admit anyone's having intellectual superiority to themselves. Society considers them intelligent but they themselves know how little they really know and how inadequate their proposed solutions are. The younger professors pretend to be sure of everything. The older professors endure the growing suspicion that they are sure of nothing.

On every large university campus there are the "walking wounded." A large number of these consist of people who once held administrative positions on the campus but have been sent back to teaching and research. The administrative jobs pay better, carry more prestige, and provide perquisites to which ordinary educators are not entitled. Some of these former administrators are victims of Peter's Principle: they reached their level of incompetence. But human beings don't like to admit their inadequacy and these people spend the rest of their lives rationalizing away their mistakes and trying to justify their blunders.

Another group of "walking wounded" consists of former administrators who are just as competent as their successors. But they made the cardinal error of helping ambitious members of their department who repaid the debt either by organizing a departmental revolt against their benefactor or by maneuvering themselves into replacing their patrons. These victims spend the rest of their careers bitterly recollecting the betrayals they suffered.

There is still another group of "walking wounded" on every campus, those whose ability as scholars or teachers is valued less highly by their colleagues and administrative superiors than by themselves. They have tenure for life. But they are stuck at one rank for the rest of their careers, with minimum increases in salary, condemned to watching younger members of the department be promoted over them, and forced to admit that the establishment considers them mediocre—totally unfair though that judgment is.

Finally, and present only for the remainder of each year, are the "walking dead," young instructors who have been denied tenure. They come to the university, eager and hopeful. They work hard and publish papers in a vast variety of journals. But if the university keeps them for seven years, the instructor gets tenure for life. In times of financial difficulty, universities do not feel secure enough to saddle themselves for twenty or thirty more years with the contract of another professor. Unless one is extraordinarily successful in publishing, the chances of getting tenure are not good. One competent young instructor is, from the university's point of view, approximately as good as another competent young instructor. So the people denied tenure walk around the campus during their final year like prisoners awaiting execution. And their tenured colleagues, feeling slightly guilty, try not to look into their eyes when they pass, and avoid in conversation the only subject that matters.

Educated people are too well informed to follow demagogues blindly. Instead, they follow demagogues knowingly—and share the same prejudices as the uneducated. The masses may be taught noble philosophies in schools, but in times of desperation, famine, or danger they react in the old familiar pattern, each for his or her own benefit. The intelligent student knows that the cliches of the classroom have little relationship to basic human interests, needs, or conditions. Although sheltered educators may recommend standards of behavior that are inapplicable to actual situations outside the school, students usually give pragmatic or cynical reasons for behavior, rarely the theoretical or idealistic motivation.

So Aldous Huxley was not indulging in a cheap witticism when he suggested that the main difference between the educated and the uneducated is that educated people are able to offer erudite reasoning to support or reject the same views that the uneducated hold or reject. There is good reason to accept the aphorism: "Learning makes a good man better and a bad man worse."

To a large extent, society gets the kind of education it deserves. In the 1930s, when the University of Chicago dropped football, President Robert Maynard Hutchins was accused of un-American activity. No one took seriously Hutchins' perfectly reasonable suggestion that the University adopt the Chicago Bears professional football team as its representative, and that other leading universities also select professional teams as their surrogates in athletic competition, permitting the universities to concentrate on education.

Educators resent the cliché, "Those who can, do; those who can't, teach; those who can't teach, teach others how to teach." Whether that statement is a vile canard or a slight exaggeration is open to dispute; certainly the reputations of most colleges of education do little to disprove the bromide.

One professor decided that his time was too valuable to waste filling out numerous forms that requested information about trivial details of his activity. So he began to fill out all questionnaires with fictitious numbers, usually carrying them at least three places beyond the decimal point. No one ever challenged his trumped-up figures, and his contributions presumably influenced the statistics eventually announced by the analysts.

When professors have taught for many years they tend to forget some of the students who have passed through their classes. But when a request for a recommendation arrives in the mail, the professor has a problem. What do you say about a person you don't remember? Some of the most imaginative writing in the country has appeared in these recommendations.

Years ago Joseph Wood Krutch anticipated the victory of graphic art. In an essay he called "Is Reading Here to Stay?" Krutch warned that book publishers must fight "the educator and the psychologist, both of whom are increasingly opposed to the printed word. . . . Perhaps in another hundred years only ideographs in the form of conventional graphs and charts will be intelligible." In a similar spirit, educators may soon require students to read material by weight instead of quality: six ounces of 5 x 8 pamphlets, for example, or four ounces of 8 1/2 x 11 booklets. That procedure would be fitting for a promotion system that already counts the number of a candidate's publications instead of evaluating the quality of the work.

Anthologies of modern literature that are used as textbooks in universities sometimes omit important literary works simply because the editors do not want to pay for copyright permissions. Anthologies of world literature often omit classics in order to avoid duplicating the anthologies of other publishers. The deprived students never learn that they were not permitted to read a great work simply because commercial considerations intervened.

The attitude toward higher education of the average American has nothing to do with scholarship. It is the athletic teams of universities that get continual publicity in the communications media. Fans know the names of football coaches at universities whose Nobel-prize-winning scientists they cannot identify. Most American males know the names of basketball and football stars at universities but cannot name a single famous scholar at any of these schools. At an alumni meeting of a leading university, a prominent sports writer asked, "When will this university learn that grades are not everything, and turn out a football team worthy of the institution?" The pep rallies before big games draw far larger crowds than meetings called to discuss important social or political crises. So it is understandable that a president of the University of Oklahoma once implored the student body to create a university that the football team could be proud of.

In universities and colleges there are teachers who inspire students to the highest level of intellectual inquiry. There are teachers who make learning a fascinating experience. There are teachers who dedicate themselves to their students, worry about them, and do all that they can to help them. But even inspiring teachers, entertaining teachers, and genuinely caring teachers are subject to social forces and psychological needs that make hypocritical behavior very difficult to avoid.

Nine

Sports

College sport "has become a business, carried on far too often by professionals, supported by levies on the public, bringing in vast receipts, demoralizing student ethics and confusing the ideals of sports, manliness, and decency."
— *Frederick Jackson Turner*

A totem is "an object or an animal that a man regards with unusual respect and to which he believes himself to stand in some intimate and special relation. . . . [The relationship] seems to be more or less mystical or supernatural."

At first glance there may seem to be no similarity between a tribesman's attitude toward his clan's totem and a sport fan's feelings about a favorite team. But some members of "primitive" communities identify so closely with their tribe's totem that they share the emotions attributed to the totem. And millions of individuals in "civilized" societies identify so closely with an athletic team that they rejoice when that team wins and suffer when that team loses.

In Europe and in South America devotees of soccer follow the fortunes of their favorite teams with wild enthusiasm. In Canada hockey brings out the fierce dedication of disciples. And in the United States football, basketball, and baseball teams have adherents whose emotional states revolve around the success and failure of their teams. An identification so strong may seem ridiculous to a sophisticated inhabitant of the Planet Earth in the twenty-first century. Nevertheless, millions of dollars are spent by American corporations every year to provide seats at athletic events for favorite and prospective customers. And Rio de Janeiro built a soccer stadium that accommodates 200,000 fans while hundreds of thousands starve in miserable ghettos.

There is an enormous popular interest in the trivia of athletics. Adults memorize the scores of games, the batting averages of players, the special achievements of athletes, and the conditions under which those achievements occurred. Not only are the great victories recorded, but the names of the losers are also perpetuated.

Statistics in the United States are kept to a preposterous extent, so that a breathless radio or television announcer can immediately inform the enormous audience that the player batting has previously hit the ball safely, with a man on second base and two outs, on Fridays, three times out of ten. Followers of horse racing, auto racing, and track subscribe to organizations that regularly provide them innumerable statistics about jockeys and horses, drivers and autos, and human beings who can move their legs more rapidly than other human beings while covering a measured distance. Adults wager millions of dollars on which man will swing a club the fewest times in order to propel a little ball into a little hole in the ground. And agile young men and women earn hundreds of thousands of dollars ferociously swinging a racket at a tennis ball and vigorously swearing at the umpires. The spectators may become so jubilant that they will generously tip nearby attendants or so perturbed that they will beat members of their own family.

The agony and the ecstasy of athletic competition have results varying from ludicrous to tragic. At American football games spectators have become so involved with the action that they ran on the field and tackled players running for a touchdown. (Excessive identification with characters in entertainments is not limited to athletics: a spectator at a performance of Othello once jumped onto the stage, yelled, "She is innocent!" and pulled Othello away as he was about to strangle Desdemona.) Men have died of heart attacks while watching exciting action in games. In taverns, drinkers get into fights over the merits of athletes and teams. In 1955 an elderly man in Pittsburgh tried to commit suicide. His explanation: the Pittsburgh Pirates kept losing. Soccer too seems to bring out suicidal tendencies. In 1978 a Mexican hanged himself after an unexpected loss to Tunisia, and a Brazilian killed himself after a tie game with Sweden. Obviously men like that were already disturbed, and the disappointment in sports was merely the final push toward suicide. But it is a revealing reflection on a society whose values are so distorted that the result of an athletic competition causes individuals to kill themselves. Most people react less violently, but it is an indisputable fact that the moods of millions of people, and their actions, are affected by athletic events.

A few years ago in the small town of Itarana in Brazil, angry fans beat to death the coach of a visiting soccer team; he had tried to prevent a player from hitting the referee. In 1985, after a soccer game in St. Gall, Switzerland, the referee and two linesmen had to be evacuated by helicopter when angry fans blocked the stadium exits. And during the World Cup in Argentina the organizers of a lecture by Jorge Luis Borges installed a television set alongside the podium, tuned silently to a soccer game. Borges never knew; he was blind. It was during the same World Cup competition that the owners of a strip-tease parlor in Buenos Aires sent away the girls and brought in television sets when the matches were televised. And it required police at the Mexico City airport to keep enraged fans away from the Mexican team that returned after three straight losses.

When an activity is as important as sports obviously are, it becomes vulnerable to machinations far removed from the ostensible purposes of the activity. Sports evolve into a business and are subject to the same manipulations and deceptions and pretenses that all businesses utilize. Sports are more guilty of hypocrisy than other business enterprises because sports have always pretended to be dedicated to other ends than making money. Sports usually pretend that their purpose is competition, not winning. When a successful football coach like Vince Lombardi admits, "Winning is not the most important thing. It's the only thing," hypocritical administrators at universities deny his statement—and dismiss their losing coaches.

Even in the earliest days of organized sports, the Olympics in ancient Greece, hypocrisy reared its charming head. In theory, athletes represented their own cities. But prize winner Croton ran for the city of Croton in his first two Olympiads and then won prizes for the richer city of Syracuse in the next two.

An obvious element of hypocrisy in sports is the pretense that sports emphasize noble qualities. Quite to the contrary, many athletes and coaches admit, as Leo Durocher did, that "nice guys finish last." It is strength, agility, determination, shrewdness, and ruthlessness that make champions, not saintliness and moral virtues. There have been, of course, athletic champions who were admirable human beings, but their success as athletes was due to qualities other than their decency. Talking about a young golfer, Gene Sarazen, one of the all-time great players, said: "I doubt that he'll win a big tournament. He is much too nice a guy. To win something like the Open, you have to be a nasty, mean, ornery buzzard just like I was." Sarazen may have overstated his case, but the point is clear. Ty Cobb and Babe Ruth did not become baseball heroes by being role models for the Boy Scouts. It is not surprising that pugnaciousness helps athletes; it is hypocritical to pretend that great athletes are motivated by morality.

The fact that certain physical characteristics are helpful in certain sports has not been ignored by sports administrators in totalitarian countries nor by entrepreneurs in free societies. Since tall men can serve a special function in basketball, tall men are being bred for basketball. Since large men satisfy a special need in football and weight lifting, men are being fattened and strengthened for football and weight lifting. And so on.

In Eastern Europe, promising children were put at a very early age into training centers that developed them into superior swimmers, gymnasts, skaters, and track performers. And in the United States some parents send their young children to live with famous coaches for years while they are prepared for careers as superior performers in sports like skating, gymnastics, and synchronized swimming. It is hard to believe that this activity reflects a high level of human destiny.

Sports are supposed to be physical activities engaged in by human bodies that developed naturally. But when athletes learned that certain drugs contribute to growth and strength they began to take advantage of these extraneous—and illegal—aids. The communist countries of Eastern Europe were suspected for a long time of using steroids and other muscle-building drugs in developing athletes for Olympic and other competitions.

These countries have always denied the use of drugs for these purposes, even when tests proved that their athletes had used these drugs. In making the denial, the communist countries were guilty of hypocrisy. But many athletes in capitalist countries also take advantage of every possible competitive edge. In most of Western Europe, in some Asian countries, and in the United States doctors are finding that some athletes are using anabolic steroids, androgenic hormones, and other strength-building substances. When these athletes, and their coaches and trainers, deny the use of drugs to enhance their performances, they are guilty of hypocrisy. By 1986 the federal government estimated that the black market in steroids exceeded $100,000,000 a year in the United States.

Among the entertaining hypocrisies that sports breed is the obvious lying indulged in by sports figures. The tremendous interest in sports has resulted in a fascination with comments by sports figures, such as coaches and prominent athletes. The euphemisms used by these speakers and the double-talk that they have perfected—interspersed, by most athletes, with "you know" after every three words—are sometimes hilarious. Sports writers who are sensitive to style often ridicule the language used by sports figures and sometimes take the trouble to interpret them to the public. The essence of the explanations is that the speaker is prevaricating.

There is no agreement among experts about the nature of aggression. Most psychologists accept, in varying degrees, the aggressive nature of man. Konrad Lorenz wrote, "There is, in the modern community, no legitimate outlet for aggressive behavior. . . . The main function of sport today lies in the cathartic discharge of aggressive urge."[1] And venerated football coach Vince Lombardi said, "I think the nature of man is to be aggressive and football is a violent game." On the other hand, anthropologist Alexander Alland, in *The Human Imperative*, insists that aggressive responses are not instinctive but are learned from one's culture. A great many "authorities" can be quoted on both sides of this controversy, enough to suggest that the disputants are really expressing their own proclivities instead of stating objective facts. And that pretense makes them guilty of hypocrisy.

It is hard to resist comparing the war dances and pre-battle rituals of "primitive" societies with the pep-meetings that precede football games on American campuses. The marching bands, cheer leaders, and violent yells might seem to a civilized observer an excessive response to athletic competition. But the tradition goes back a very long way.

Ever since the Olympic Games began in 776 BC, athletic champions have been treated as heroes by men and as irresistible lovers by women. In *The Olympic Games: The First Thousand Years,* M. I. Finley and H. W. Picket show that the ancient Olympics had many problems that plague modern games. There were difficulties with cheating, exorbitant costs, and national rivalries. Alexander the Great refused to compete, except against other kings. King Herod of Judea contributed heavily to the endowment of the Olympics, was named an honorary Greek, and served as President of the Games. And Emperor Nero introduced two new events so he could win: a musical contest and a ten-horse chariot race.

It is a revealing fact that boxing, wrestling, and free-style fighting were the most brutal events in the Olympic program—and, next to the chariot races, the most popular. Konrad Lorenz's remarks are relevant: "Human sport is more akin to serious fighting than animal play. . . . also, sport indubitably contains aggressive motivation, demonstrably absent in most animal play."[2]

To deny that the popularity of sports is based on aggression is to deny the obvious— and to be hypocritical. The largest gate-receipts in the United States come from heavyweight boxing matches. Professional wrestling orchestrates the kinds of violence its actors perform. There have been occasions when brawls and crowd fights have been arranged by executives of professional hockey to stimulate attendance at subsequent matches. And in Dubuque, Iowa, the School Board refused to discipline a high-school football coach who allowed a chicken to be kicked by team members. The coach explained that he used the chicken as a gimmick to inspire his players in preparation for a game against a team nick-named "Golden Warriors." The chicken had been spray-painted gold.

The popularity of bull fighting is often explained by aficionados as admiration for grace under pressure—an aesthetic experience. But in *La Fiesta Brava* Barnaby Conrad writes, The brave bull is "the most perfect living instrument for killing that man can devise." Conrad adds a practical observation: "A bullfighter doesn't eat before a performance so that he can be operated on immediately if he is gored; if he must be gored, he hopes it will be in Madrid, where specialists in such surgery are concentrated."

Even in its earliest days, athletic competition and pure amateurism did not blend. But it was not until the twentieth century that the owners of professional teams went to such lengths as changing the size of a baseball park to accommodate the special skills of a batter they had acquired, or to slant the base lines to help a fast team bunt. Other owners wet the base paths to slow up an opposing team that is known for its speed. Far from enjoying the thrill of meeting an unfamiliar opponent, coaches send scouts to observe future rivals and record in minute detail their technique and style. Professional scouting organizations provide their special services to teams willing to pay them. Some teams send spies to watch their opponents' preparations for games.

Totalitarian countries, as we have seen, made it part of national policy to subsidize promising children and train them until they became world-class athletes. In the United States, professional basketball teams—and some university teams—select specified players not for their basketball-playing proficiency but for their ability to intimidate and injure opposing players. Sometimes the "intimidator" is proudly identified by his team. The relationship between this kind of brutality and the expressed purposes of athletics is somewhat obscure, but surely no hypocrisy is involved.

A year before South Korea was to serve as host for the Olympics it demonstrated clearly the nature of sports in modern society. The following item is reprinted verbatim (*Des Moines Register,* June 5, 1987):

> South Korea's top woman track star says she doesn't blame her coach for beating her during a training session because, she says, it will improve their relationship. Lim Chun-ae was hospitalized with a fractured

ear drum this week after Coach Kim Pon-il beat her during a weekend training session for poor times. "I don't blame Coach Kim for what happened," Lim said. "I blame myself for not having done my best to improve my record. He made me what I am." Korean athletic officials said such incidents were not unusual and coaches sometimes beat or paddle athletes to encourage them to train harder.

Although most amateur athletics are not fixed, from time to time scandals reveal that players have performed less skillfully than they were capable of performing, in exchange for money or drugs or other considerations. The administrators of universities where these scandals appear always express shock—and continue to dismiss honest coaches who fail to win as many games as the school and its alumni would like to win. The owners of professional teams complain that the salaries paid athletes are absurdly high—and then pay absurdly higher salaries to lure players away from other teams.

Not all the hypocrisies of sport are vicious. Some are simply amusing. One coach of a college basketball team had a player climb on the shoulders of a team-mate to take a shot; the coach was illustrating the over-emphasis on tall players, but no one paid any attention to him. Runners who are unlikely to win serve as mechanical rabbits for their team-mates, setting a fast pace, then dropping out of the race. A successful football coach at an eastern university told his lonesome football players, "Forget about the girl back home. I'll get you married to a rich girl." Some of his players married wealthy women. It is legal to bet on horses at race tracks but, in most states, illegal to bet on horses anywhere else. The logic of this escapes the average mind. But surely no hypocrisy is involved.

Making sports a surrogate religion is sacrilegious, demeaning, and hypocritical. But several scholars have suggested that for a great many people today, sports gratify the emotional needs that religion is supposed to serve. Catholic lay theologian Michael Novak wrote, in *The Joy of Sports,* that the rituals of sport provide "an experience of at least a pagan sense of godliness. Among the godward signs in contemporary life, sports may be the single most powerful manifestation."

In a 1983 study of Brazilian sports called "Soccer Madness," Janet Lever speculated that sporting spectacles "belong to the world of the sacred rather than the profane; fans who say sport provides an escape from 'real life' in effect sustain this religious distinction. . . . Like the effect of a religious celebration, sport fosters a sense of identification with the others who shared the experience."

In a paper he presented at the annual meeting of the Society for the Scientific Study of Religion, sociologist James Mathisen claimed that the Super Bowl has become "the American spectacle of folk religion. . . the festival of the folk, their faith, their practice, and their history." Mathisen suggests that sports filled the emotional gap suffered by Americans after the Vietnam War, when the conviction that God is on our side could not be easily sustained. The emergence of sports as the common religion was aided enormously by the tendency of television to create sports heroes and magnify the importance of sports events.

Mathisen goes on to say: "As an American, I simply am expected to be a 'generic' sports fan and possibly also have a favorite team or alma mater that becomes a community with which I identify and a clan whose symbols and totems bind me to it. . . . Being a sports fan is comparable to being religious—it's a taken-for-granted, American thing to do." The Halls of Fame that the major American sports have created, says Mathisen, evoke tradition and history in a manner similar to that of religion. And the minute records of sports history function in the same way as the "sacred writings and the historical accounts of any religious group, providing a timeless, informative guide by which later disciples' accomplishments are judged."

In 1906 Frederick Jackson Turner, an eminent American historian, made a speech that sounds surprisingly modern. Among the statements in that lecture are the following:

> [College sport] has become a business, carried on far too often by professionals, supported by levies on the public, bringing in vast receipts, demoralizing student ethics and confusing the ideals of sport, manliness and decency. . . . Coaches and managers scour the country for material. . . . Faculties are deceived into certifying the eligibility of mercenaries, and the faculty cloak is made to cover the evil practices. . . . The public has pushed its influence inside the college walls, and is demoralizing student sentiment, exalting fictitious heroes, condoning brutality, setting up false ideas of the true honor of a university.[3]

One incident that may have contributed to Professor Turner's indignation occurred during the previous year, 1905. At the football game in Iowa City between the University of Iowa and Iowa State College, the local students found a steam engine with a three-tone whistle. When the ISC students had the ball, the U of I students tied open the whistle with a rope, releasing a blast that continued throughout the series of downs. The noise was so loud that the quarterback had to tell the signals to each player individually. Not until the University of Iowa had won the game did the home town officials remove the steam whistle.

The University of Alabama built a reputation as a football power over the years. In 1987, when the president of the university selected a new coach who had a reputation for emphasizing academic performance, both the president and the new coach received death threats serious enough to require police protection. The president admitted to the press that by sending the message that Alabama would no longer be "a football factory" he was "putting his own job on the line."

Financially lucrative sports and amateurism have proved to be incompatible. In the days of the ancient Olympiads, champions were proselytized and rewarded by undercover gifts, patronage of wealthy sponsors, special privileges, and sexual favors. Periodically, the sports pages in the United States expose the scandalous behavior of universities in paying prospective football and basketball players to attend their universities. Money is given, autos are provided, compliant women students are made available, jobs for family members are found, and so on. The presidents of universities always seem surprised when the violations are revealed. Since some of these athletes, from poor families, drive convertibles on the campus, live in comfortable apartments, wear expensive clothing, and spend money freely, the ignorance of the university presidents is suspect—and the possibility of hypocrisy is present.

At the leading football universities in the U. S., the salaries of the head football coaches far exceed the salaries of university presidents.

When cheating by college athletes is revealed, their coaches express shock. The coaches are not shocked by the cheating they themselves regularly indulge in while they recruit the same athletes. It startles the coaches to learn that a young man who has been illegally rewarded by them should himself engage in illegal behavior. What coaches mean by "building character" and what athletes demonstrate by their behavior rarely coincide.

A visitor from another galaxy, who had been told that the purpose of universities is higher education, may be surprised to learn that winning teams elicit greater contributions of money from alumni and losing teams result in lower financial response. It may seem absurd to reduce the budget of a chemistry department because a young man from another state did not throw the football accurately while he wore this university's uniform, but such is the sad fact. It is difficult for the man in the street to believe that Johns Hopkins University, the University of Chicago, MIT, and Caltech really are prestigious educational institutions without fielding powerful teams in athletics.

Since the television networks pay large sums for the privilege of televising university games, they have also assumed control of the game to the extent of changing dates and starting times, and calling arbitrary times-out in order to present commercial messages. It is not too much to expect that the television networks and the advertising agencies will invent new games in which the compliant universities will be happy to engage, having long ago abandoned the pretense of being educational institutions and admitted their new mission as training camps and minor leagues for professional sports.

But one thing the public can rely on. Hypocrisy will prevail. The usurpation of college athletics by commercial interests will be presented and publicized as a splendid example of amateurism, nobility, and altruism. An oxymoron is a figure of speech that is self-contradictory, such as bittersweet, make haste slowly, and giant shrimp. Another oxymoron in modern America is the term student-athlete.

Ten

Aesthetics

*In art, "styles change for reasons of fashion, just
as they do in other worlds."*
—Tom Wolfe

If there are permanent, universal criteria for
judging art, persons who understand these criteria have the right to apply them to individual
works of art and artistic performances. If, on the
other hand, there are no permanent or universal standards, then the judgments rendered by
critics are severely restricted by geography, time,
parochialism, or purely subjective elements.

In every art there is a level of technical skill
that an artist must reach before he or she is considered a professional. Practitioners in each art

and experts associated with each art are qualified to recognize performance at a professional level. (This eliminates the person who says, "I don't know anything about art, but I know what I like.") But above the level of talented performance, there is no objective test. That is why there is disagreement every year among the practitioners who choose the best movies of the year, the best performances of the year, and the best musical achievements of the year. That is why there is disagreement among critics who select the best novel of the year, the best play, the best poetry, the best history, and the best biography. *Citizen Kane* did not win an Oscar, nor did several of the best actors and actresses ever receive one.

The variety of human tastes in aesthetics is wryly demonstrated in the 27 Canons of Beauty set by the medieval Moresco:[1]

> Three white: skin, teeth, hands
> Three black: eyes, eye lashes, eyebrows
> Three red: lips, cheeks, nails
> Three long: body, hair, hands
> Three short: ears, teeth, chin
> Three wide: breast, forehead, space between eyes
> Three narrow: waist, hands, feet
> Three thin: fingers, ankles, nostrils
> Three plump: lips, arms, hips

Every one of these canons is contradicted by one culture or another and in Western culture at one time or another. It is hypocritical to pretend that there is a single universal standard of female beauty. If there is, it certainly is not accepted by those tribes in West Africa and in the South Pacific who deliberately fatten young women to make them more attractive.

Thoreau wrote, "Inventions are likely to be improved means to unimproved ends." How right he was. Television transmits, smoothly and colorfully, the appallingly mediocre programs that it purveys. The adaptation of classical literature for television or film presentation sometimes resembles painting the Mona Lisa pink because pink is the fashionable color that season. Thoreau would have to change the adjective in another of his statements: "The mass of men lead lives of quiet desperation." Certainly there is no silence in the lives of adults who ride on music-filled elevators, sit at public events next to spectators with transistor radios, or await replies on music-playing telephones. It is worth considering Mencken's statement: "No one ever went broke underestimating the taste of the American public." It is hypocritical to pretend that these technical innovations have not lowered the standards of entertainment.

The criticism of literature, music, and art in the Western world shows enormous changes of criteria. During the last three centuries every new form of music was viciously attacked and resisted by contemporary musicians and critics, even when the new music was created by Beethoven, Wagner, and Schoenberg. But in each of the subsequent generations, the music of Beethoven, Wagner, and Schoenberg was vehemently defended against the innovators of the latest generation. New music—Baroque or Classical or Romantic—is always ridiculed. The previously castigated kind of music is defended with fanatical fervor and intensity, until a new form is accepted. Even Plato wrote, "Musical innovation is dangerous to the State, for when modes of music change, the laws of the state always change with them."[2]

Some years ago Deems Taylor, a prominent musician and critic, described an experience he had just had. He came late to a concert of new music, and he identified the works by the titles on the program he had been given; as each piece was played, he nodded in agreement. Suddenly he realized that the concert was over—and he was expecting to hear one more work. Having come in late, he had not known that what he thought was the first piece listed on the program was actually the second piece, and so on through the entire concert. But the eminent critic had persuaded himself as he listened that there was an actual relationship between the titles he saw listed and the music that he was hearing.

In a recent book, architect Peter Blake belittles almost every concept of modern building design that people take for granted. Building high tower that are raised off the ground on columns so that pedestrians can circulate freely through wide open spaces, parks, and playgrounds, is a concept of city planning widely recommended in architecture schools. The attempt to execute that concept has failed as far as the inhabitants of those areas are concerned. The use of glass draped over steel or concrete frames is a popular architectural practice. In fact, all-glass buildings have created enormous problems for themselves and for their neighbors. Large high-rise housing developments for families with children proliferated in the latter half of the twentieth century and have proved to be, in alarming numbers, disasters. The idea that prefabrication solves most building problems has not worked; prefabrication emphasizes standardization without lowering prices enough to justify the process. It is hypocritical to pretend that modern architecture is entirely successful.

The absurdities of modern art are familiar enough. A *New Yorker* cartoon shows a dog in an art gallery pulling his master towards a painting in which grotesque blots and lines are labeled "Dog." In 1985 Sotheby's announced that it was planning to auction "a slightly futuristic oil painting done by a three-year-old orangutan named Sid during his 'blue period.'" The spokesman for Sotheby's said, "The art field widens all the time. This could be the beginning of a new era." And in 1974, at a Mississippi art competition, an Afghan hound won the top prize in the weaving category for an old mitten that he had chewed up. The mitten had been entered in the competition under the dog's name, Alexis Boyar, by its owner, who described the work as a "small fiber wall hanging in off-white, with a range of interesting textures and a central phallic shape." On a number of occasions, the splotchings perpetrated by monkeys have won awards in art competitions.

James McNeill Whistler was ridiculed by the leading art critic of England, John Ruskin. In the famous court case against Ruskin, the jury awarded Whistler a contemptuous award of one farthing. But today Whistler is revered and Ruskin is denigrated.

In literature, at one time or another, Classicism, Romanticism, Impressionism, and Expressionism have been accepted as desirable norms and rejected as obnoxious abnormalities. The changes in painting range from naive realism to fantastic abstractions, sometimes within a single decade. And the hypocritical critics, out of ignorance, inadequacy, or neurosis, keep insisting that only Style X is acceptable and Style Z is totally reprehensible—at the moment.

Poetry prizes have been awarded to pranksters who later admitted that they had concocted the poems by pasting together random lines from newspapers. The Polish satirist Stanislaw Lec published a book entitled: "A Perfect Vacuum: Perfect Reviews of Nonexistent Books." Victor Hugo announced that the six greatest writers were Homer, Aeschylus, Isaiah, Juvenal, Dante, and Shakespeare, and that he was the seventh. And a Latin verse quoted in *The Anatomy of Melancholy* says:[3]

> No verses can please men or live long
> That are written by water-drinkers.

There is no lack of mistakes made by critics. One scholar wrote an impressive paper on Melville's brilliant use of the phrase "soiled serpents of the deep" in Moby Dick. But a later reading of Melville's manuscript revealed that Melville had written "coiled serpents." A similar misunderstanding occurred in a college classroom: the professor quoted Hawthorne's note in his *Journal*, "That foul cavern, the human heart." In the next examination, a student wrote: "That foul tavern, the human heart."

The conventional interpretation of Kafka's *The Trial* sees the book as a symbol of humanity's fate. But Ronald Hayman's biography says that Kafka himself called *The Trial* a description of the cross-examination he had just been subjected to by his fiancée and her best friend (at the moment pregnant by Kafka).

Several "bibles" of literary criticism have had only brief periods of acceptance. In the 1930's William Empson's *Seven Types of Ambi-*

guity was required reading for every literary critic. But a few years later the book lost its influence and a scholar wrote, "The celebrated seven types proved in the long run a set of distinctions without differences." Similarly, in the 1950s Northrop Frye's *Anatomy of Criticism* had to be read by every doctoral candidate in literature. But when professors found that students totally disagreed in their attempts to apply Frye's theories to specific works of literature, the book became only a stimulating example of original thinking.

Sometimes the qualities of a literary work have nothing to do with aesthetic intentions. For instance, Dr. Emmett F. Pearson, a physician, offers a reasonable explanation for the brevity of Lincoln's *Gettysburg Address*. On the day he delivered the address, Lincoln was suffering from fever. "If he didn't feel well," says Dr. Pearson, "he wasn't going to write a long speech." Nor were purely literary criteria applied when the Attorney General of Massachusetts tried to have *Forever Amber* banned in his state. In the court case he presented the following list to support his argument that the novel was obscene, "Seventy references to sexual intercourse; thirty-nine illegitimate pregnancies; seven abortions; ten descriptions of women dressing, undressing, or bathing in the presence of men; five references to incest; ten references ridiculing marriage; and the references to women's bosoms and other parts of their anatomy were so numerous I did not even attempt to count them."[4] The court did not find the book obscene.

In 1976, as part of the celebration of its seventy-fifth anniversary, the *London Times Literary Supplement* asked a large number of critics, artists, and scholars to name the most underrated and overrated books and authors of the past seventy-five years. The results of this poll are both contradictory and revealing. Named most frequently as overrated: Arnold Toynbee ("neither history nor a study"); James Joyce ("arrogant, unpleasant, and above all, quite unreadable"); George Orwell; Ezra Pound; Virginia Woolf; T.E. Lawrence; André Malraux; Teilhard de Chardin; Hannah Arendt; André Gide; Herman Hesse; E.M. Forster; Alexander Solzhenitsyn; Iris Murdoch; Kurt Vonnegut; Saul Bellow; Leo Tolstoy ("Anna Karenina is sheer nonsense"). The "underrated" writers included Ring Lardner, John O'Hara, H.G. Wells, Karl Jung, Barbara Pym, Jocelyn Brooke, and the authors of the Bible.

At a seminar on literary criticism two well-known scholars took opposing positions. Both of them were intelligent, well-read, reasonable men. Meeting at a party a few months later, each admitted that he had come around to accepting the view of his antagonist that he had deprecated at the seminar.

The criteria of art are not absolute. At any time in recent history, and today, one can choose from different journals, books, and public lectures contradictory opinions by critics of music, literature, art, theater, film, and architecture. The public radio network in the United States for a long time featured a program on which leading critics evaluated new recordings of musical classics. Invariably, these experts disagreed vehemently in their judgments of these recordings. Reviewers of new movies often differ enormously in their critiques. And the evaluations of modern paintings are so inconsistent as to approach absurdity.

Writing in 1987 George Seldes recalled his reaction to the performances of Sara Bernhardt he had witnessed in 1910. "I still remember that at the time I thought every word, every gesture was sublime." But in 1980 a friend sent Seldes a cassette with the voice of Bernardt. Seldes writes:

> Immediately I realized that what was divine in 1910 is "ham" in 1980. The divinity of the earliest decade of the century is shouting, ranting, emoting, in the ninth decade . . . if the Divine Sara were to appear in New York today in *L'Aiglon,* every critic in the metropolis would describe her as a "ham actress", or at best "a very old-fashioned actress."[5]

There is a good deal of evidence to support Tom Wolfe's thesis that all aesthetic judgments reflect current fads and that all these judgments are relative. The critic, Wolfe claims, is merely responding to the contemporary, and ephemeral, values of his colleagues, either by conforming to those values or by attacking them. All aesthetic judgments, Wolfe argues, are simply reflections of current vogues and fashions, temporary values, and pitiful attempts to be *au courant*. "Art is the religion of the educated classes," says Wolfe. ". . . styles [in art] change for reasons of fashion, just as they do in other worlds."

The problem of who is qualified to be a critic is a very old one. On the one hand, what right do people who do not create art, namely critics, have to criticize? On the other hand, one may know what should be done even if he or she cannot do it. Many teachers, coaches, and advisers have demonstrated that. Universities offer courses in aesthetics and scholars write books on the nature of art, but there is no consensus on what art is or how it should be evaluated. Nor does the future offer any promises; computers cannot judge art. Spengler was not the first, and will not be the last, to comment on the conflict between science and aesthetics. It is not surprising that a prominent drama critic, Kenneth Tynan, wrote, "A critic is a man who knows the way but can't drive the car."[6]

In 1846 Kirkegaard wrote, "Soon the only thing people will read will be gossip." What passes for drama on television today would make the Danish theologian gag. But one cannot legislate morality or taste. Adults have the right to read comic books if they want to, just as they have the right to keep wearing diapers if they choose to do so. There are significant differences between the art produced for the sole purpose of entertainment, the art created for the purpose of self-expression, and the art intended to convey profound insights. But these varieties of art overlap in intention and in result. Self-expression sometimes proves to be entertaining, sometimes profound. Entertaining art sometimes reveals deep insight. And "serious" art always involves self-expression and sometimes results in entertainment.

In a review of Stanley Kubrick's movie, *A Clockwork Orange*, based on Anthony Burgess's novel, the art critic of *TIME* wrote,

> At issue is the popular nineteenth century idea, still held today, that Art is Good for You, that the purpose of the fine arts is to provide moral uplift. Kubrick's message . . . is the opposite: art has no ethical purpose. Art serves . . . to promote ecstatic consciousness. The kind of ecstasy depends on the person who is having it. Without the slightest contradiction, Nazis would weep over Wagner before stoking the crematoriums.[7]

So much has been written about art that the seeker of certainty becomes surfeited. Still,

Jacques Barzun's remarks are worth considering:

> Like philosophy, but clothed in seductive forms, art records man's consciousness about life and death. Appearance and Reality are the main concern of both artist and philosopher. . . . The awareness of death gives the philosopher his idea of an absolute in experience; the consciousness of life gives the artist the materials for his deliberate relativism. Man as philosopher keeps seeking for the one absolute philosophy, whereas man as artist keeps multiplying relative points of view, which we find in the varied and opposing schools of art.[8]

Critics have a right to express opinions on a work of art or an artistic performance. They have no right to pretend that those opinions are based on absolute standards. To that extent, most criticism is hypocritical.

Eleven

Religion

The Bible
Can be read in such a way
As to permit the atomic bomb.
                    —Japanese poet Gyoten

In many obvious ways religion is guilty of hypocrisy. Most religions require noble and altruistic behavior on the part of their clergy and their worshippers. The teachings of Jesus, for example, demand a virtuousness that few human beings have been able to maintain. To the extent that members of a religious community fail to practice the precepts of their religion, but pretend to be practicing those precepts, the clergy and the congregations are being hypocritical.

The more noticeable forms of hypocrisy in religion are familiar to everyone. Priests, ministers, rabbis, mullahs, monks, and nuns are human beings as well as religious functionaries. They are subject to the same desires, conflicts, weaknesses, and needs that all human beings experience. But when religious individuals fall short of perfection, or contradict the lofty teachings of their faith, the failure seems much more reprehensible and the hypocrisy much more despicable, than similar transgressions on the part of the secular community.

Religious institutions are subject to the same social pressures and requirements—financial needs, deterioration of buildings, competition for clients, necessity of a good public image—that other institutions face. But when religious institutions fall short of absolute propriety, and thus contradict the teachings of their faith, the defect seems more nefarious and the hypocrisy more contemptible than identical violations on the part of secular institutions. This unequal treatment of the clergy and ecclesiastic institutions may be unfair, but it indisputably exists.

The hypocrisy of religious individuals is demonstrated in various forms. Religions traditionally support "the establishment." Religions almost always justify the wars waged by their own countries and claim that God is on their side even when Christians fight Christians,

Muslims fight Muslims, and Buddhists fight Buddhists.

One source of hypocrisy is the obvious contradiction between the love most religions preach and the violence many believers practice. History shows overwhelming evidence of the ease with which religious leaders convince their followers that warfare, murder, brutality, and exploitation are permissible against the followers of other religions and against their own co-religionists who interpret the teachings of their religion slightly differently from the way they do. Some historians claim that more people have died as a result of religious wars than for any other reason.

In general terms, this contradiction between expressed love and practiced hatred has always been known. But a book by René Girard, *Violence and the Sacred,* draws on Biblical scripture, structural anthropology, psychoanalysis, Greek myth, African ritual, and many other sources to demonstrate that violence pervades all sacred institutions and rests at the very foundation of religion.

It is not surprising that Robert Burns wrote:
Morality, thou deadly bane,
Thy tens of thousands thou has slain.

Relying on years of experience as an Anglican clergyman, Jonathan Swift said, "We have just enough religion to make us hate, but not enough to make us love, one another."

Summarizing his three-volume *History of the Crusades*, Stephen Runciman wrote,

> It was not so much wickedness as stupidity that ruined the Holy Wars. . . . There was so much courage and so little honor, so much devotion and so little understanding. High ideals were besmirched by cruelty and greed, enterprise and endurance by a blind and narrow self-righteousness; and the Holy War itself was nothing more than a long act of intolerance in the name of God, which is the sin against the Holy Ghost.

Common to most religions is the repeated claim that if everyone became religious, peace would come to earth. Actually, the opposite claim can be made with the support of history. (The other traditional cause of wars, economic expansion, is usually camouflaged under the guise of religion or patriotism.) When the Church in Europe was most powerful, in such periods as the fourteenth century for instance, there were more wars between Catholic countries than ever. After the Reformation, brutal wars repeatedly occurred between Catholics and Protestants. Massacres were not limited to Huguenots. The bitterness between Muslims and Christians is clearly demonstrated in places where those religions have existed side by side for a long time, as in Cyprus and Lebanon.

The opposing argument is even more hypocritical: people without religion, like Nazis and

Communists, have proved to be even more brutal and pugnacious than the exponents of peace and love. And it is one of the familiar ironies of history that the Puritans, who fled England to obtain religious freedom, immediately denied that freedom to everyone else as soon as they established themselves in America.

During the American war in Vietnam, a study of church profits from the war was made by the Corporate Information Center of the National Council of Churches. The study concluded that the investment policies of the churches did not match their expression of moral concern; instead, they had put themselves "in a position of moral complicity." Ten major Protestant denominations had investments of 203 million dollars in prime military contractors. "These investments are big business for the churches, representing an important if not the most important portion of their holdings." Among the items manufactured by the church-supported corporations were bombers, missiles, guns, antipersonnel mines, rockets, and tanks.

The Hebrew Bible teaches, "Thou shalt not kill." Jesus preached, "Love thy neighbor as thyself." The illogical extension of these injunctions became the slogan, among some fundamentalists and conservative Christians, "Kill a commie for Christ."

Religious aggression, of course, is not limited to Christians. An ancient proverb from Buddhist Sri Lanka tells us, "Even priests who live in the same temple have arguments."

Another source of hypocrisy in religion is fear of the unknown. As infants, human beings are usually taken care of by seemingly omniscient and omnipotent adults who protect them and plan for them. Many people, after they grow up, expand this trust into the comforting belief that a powerful supernatural being, somewhere, continues to look out for them and to oversee the operation of the universe. It is very hard for most people to consider the possibility that no one is concerned with their individual welfare and no one is arranging the destinies of humankind.

Bernard Shaw ridiculed the popular notion of God as "Everybody's Big Papa" but Proust admitted, "When we see ourselves on the edge of the abyss and it seems God has abandoned us, we no longer hesitate to expect a miracle."[1] William Bolitho speaks of "that eternal legatee of lost hopes, the Church."[2] A. E. Housman's lines are relevant:

> I, a stranger and afraid,
> In a world I never made.

Alfred Whitehead adds a twentieth-century philosopher's suspicion that God may be changing all the time. Then, of course, there is Nietzsche's suggestion that God is dead, offset somewhat by religionists' irrefutable observation that Nietzsche is dead.

Mencken's reasoning in *Treatise on the Gods* follows the traditional rationale of skeptics: all religions stem from fear of the unknown, all religions are illusions. Buddhism advocates the suppression of worldly desires in order to avoid the disappointment of failure; one cannot regret the lack of something one does not want. Buddha and Christ taught that the only way to win the world was to lose all desire to win it, but most human beings want the pleasure of winning and find the literal practice of Buddhism and Christianity an unbearable restriction on human behavior.

Hypocrisy in religion appears in other ways. When an empty church burns down, divine intervention is praised for preventing loss of congregational lives. But catastrophes that strike occupied houses of worship and seminary dormitories are dismissed as inexplicable.

In one form or another, human beings return to religion because there is no place else to go. They have so little control of their own destinies and of the fates of those they cherish that the inclination to ask some powerful force for help is almost irresistible. But, just as the laws of nature require a reaction to every action, the laws of religion demand payment for divine help: a prescribed kind of behavior. In the failure to follow that behavior, and in attempts to avoid following it, hypocrisy prevails.

Another source of hypocrisy in religion is the pretense of knowing more than one actually knows. As Cardinal Newman freely admitted, religion is based on faith, not on reason. But one person's faith is another person's superstition. Christianity, Islam, and Judaism refuse to grant to animism and African witchcraft the same validity that they claim for their own religions. Yet the major religions of the world, on one hand, and the hundreds of bizarre cults, on the other, all rely on suppositions that cannot be empirically tested or scientifically demonstrated.

Eminent sociologists try to explain religion in objective terms. Emil Durkheim, for example, suggests that different concepts of God are thinly disguised self-images of different societies. If Durkheim is right, each of these images is a pretense, and pretense is hypocrisy. Max Weber concluded that elementary religions turn to the supernatural for the pragmatic rewards of long life, sufficient food, defeat of enemies, and avoidance of catastrophes. The motivations of advanced religions are simply more sophisticated versions of the same desires.

"He was a wise man who invented God," Plato said. Much later Voltaire wrote, "If God did not exist, it would be necessary to invent him." But invented gods fail to impress some philosophers. In *Soliloquies in England* Santayana wrote, "My atheism, like that of Spinoza, is true piety toward the universe and denies only gods fashioned by men in their own image, to be servants of their human interests."

Not all societies believe in high gods. Today millions of people, particularly in China, Japan, and much of Eastern Europe, are essentially atheistic. A recent study by Whiting showed that only a third of the hunter-gatherer societies he surveyed worshipped omnipotent supernatural beings. The concept of God as a shepherd, in the Judeo-Christian model, is most likely to originate in a society dependent on herding, and that god is always male, as herding is essentially a male task. "The enduring paradox of religion," concludes Edward O. Wilson, "is that so much of its substance is demonstrably false, yet it remains a driving force in all societies. Men would rather believe than know."[3]

Every religion tends to assume that only its faith is the right one, and all others are mistaken. Ambrose Bierce recognized this propensity in his definition of the Bible: "Scriptures. The sacred books of our holy religion, as distinguished from the false and profane writings on which all other faiths are based." In 900 BC the Greek gods numbered about 30,000; to make sure that no god was angered by omission, the Greeks observed a Feast of the Unknown Gods.[4]

Although many adherents of the major religions think that they are unique in recommending the Golden Rule, the fact is that every widely accepted religion pretends to abide by this precept and shares the hypocrisy of failing to practice it. The Hebrew Bible taught: "What is hurtful to yourself, do not do to your fellow man." Jesus said, "All things that men should do to you, do you to them." Confucius put it like this: "Do not do unto others what you would not they should do unto you." Buddha preached, "Hurt not others with that which hurts you." Hinduism: "This is the sum of duty—do nothing to others that, if done to you, would cause you pain." The Taoists say, "Regard your neighbor's gain as your own gain; and your neighbor's loss as your own loss." Zoroaster said, "That nature only is good that does not do unto another what is not good for its own self." And Islam teaches, "No one of you is a believer until he loves for his brother what he loves for himself."

The refusal of religions to admit their ignorance is, of course, hypocritical. The unwillingness of religions to acknowledge contradictions in their behavior is hypocritical. The Catholic Church does not permit priests to marry now. But at one time it accepted the marriages of priests. The Church at one time made Galileo retract his statement that the Earth was not the center of the universe; today the Church agrees with the rest of educated humanity on this subject. Before 1908 the Church of England condemned the use of birth control; now the Church accepts it. At one time the Church of England forbade cremation; now the procedure is permitted. (Catholics too could not be cremated until a ruling issued by the Pope in 1963 sanctioned the process.) Orthodox Jews cannot be cremated; Conservative and Reformed Jews can.

For more than a century after its founding, the Mormon Church did not permit Blacks to become priests. Recently a change in policy was announced after a revelation from God. The announcement did not say who received the revelation, or explain the manner in which it was received. Nor did the announcement make reference to the increasing protests of Blacks against the discrimination that the previous rules of the church imposed on them, nor to the expanding proselytizing efforts by Mormon missionaries in Africa, Asia, and South America. God changed His mind and is now willing to accept Blacks as Mormon priests.

Observers in the Western world are not the only ones who have been puzzled by apparent inconsistencies in the management of a divinely operated universe. In the fifteenth century a Chinese poet, Hsieh Chin, commented on some anomalies:

Apologia

In vain hands bent on sacrifice
or clasped in prayer we see;
The ways of God are not exactly
what those ways should be.
The swindler and the ruffian
lead pleasant lives enough,
While judgments overtake the good
and many a sharp rebuff. . . .

And if great God Almighty fails
to keep the balance true,
What can we hope that paltry mortal
magistrates will do?

Hsieh Chin (1369-1415),
trans., Herbert A. Giles

Religions make the unprovable assumption that beyond the apparent unfairness of life there is justice after death and a satisfying reward for those who qualify. The tendency to imagine Heaven in terms of earthly comfort is quite understandable. Different heavens provide for different expectations of Heaven. The Roman Catholic Church, for instance, reserves the lowest level of Hell for suicides; but Shinto claims that Japanese who commit the proper kind of suicide spend eternity in the highest section of Heaven.

Although in all religions some kind of Heaven is provided, the particular architecture and the type of bliss differ considerably. Mark Twain ridiculed the conventional form of the

Christian Heaven, the boredom of eternal hymn singing, and the characteristics of the inhabitants. Twain expressed his own preference for Hell. The Roman Catholic Church teaches that many souls have to pass through Purgatory before they are permitted to enter Heaven. Other Christian denominations also believe that a period of punishment or expiation is required before most souls achieve divine bliss.

In popular versions of Islamic Heaven, material delights are abundantly provided. Paradise, for example, offers delights of the flesh; but some Muslim scholars insist that these passages are allegorical and the follower of Allah who expects to spend eternity with houris and wine is doomed to disappointment. The Japanese version of Heaven also satisfies sexual desires and provides gourmet chefs and skilled bartenders. The Jewish Heaven is rather bland and dull, if it exists.

Ancient Greek religion offered the Elysian fields, a happy otherworld for heroes favored by the gods. It was located in the distant west, at the edge of the world. In a later tradition, Elysium was part of the underworld and a pleasant abode for the righteous dead. In classical and Celtic legend, the Fortunate Islands or Islands of the Blessed were situated in the Western Ocean. There, the souls of lucky mortals were received by the gods and existed happily.

In Norse mythology, Valhalla was a martial paradise to which beautiful Valkyrie brought slain warriors. Zoroaster taught that every person, after death, crosses the Bridge of the Separator, which spans Hell; for the evil individual the bridge narrows, tossing him or her into Hell; but the good person finds a wide road to the Realm of Light. Since temperature affects one's comfort, young missionaries in Alaska were advised not to mention hell-fire to the Eskimos. When the first preachers told them about the heat in hell, some Eskimos expressed a desire to go there immediately.

The ancient Egyptian version of Osiris's kingdom was sensuous: full of slaves, rich food, ornate clothing, jewelry. The Christian notion includes golden streets, a profusion of harps, gilded wings. The Nirvana of Hinduism is restrained: union with God offers such serenity that no physical distractions are necessary. American Indians looked forward to a Happy Hunting Ground where no White conservation officers interfered.

The Judeo-Christian tradition has identified a large number of angels (according to medieval Jewish scholars, 301,655,722), bodiless spirits who stand midway in the chain between God and man. In *A Dictionary of Angels* Gustav Davidson includes brief biographies of 3,406 angels whose names, characteristics, and activities are recorded in the Bible, Kabbalist and rabbinical writings, works of the church fathers, and poetry. The Bible mentions only three angels by names. Michael, holder of the keys to Heaven, led God's army in the victorious battle with Satan's wicked supporters. Gabriel presides over paradise and, according to Allah, dictated the Koran to Muhammad. Raphael is ruling prince of the Second Heaven. Another important angel, not mentioned in the Bible, is Uriel, archangel of Salvation, who warned Noah of the Flood.

Some angels were mischievous. According to the Jewish Kabbalah, the angel Balthazar specializes in such pranks as stealing women's garters, and the angel Vassago can be appealed to when one wants to learn a woman's secrets. Medieval Christian theologians conducted lengthy and heated debates over the pressing problem of how many angels can dance on the head of a pin. With the development of the modern computer, that dispute should be resolved very soon.

Although it may seem illogical, polls indicate that many more Americans believe in Heaven than in Hell. It is not hard to explain the discrepancy on grounds of wishful thinking, which has been known to disregard logic. Hells vary among different religions and in different cultures. The Hades of ancient Greeks was gloomy, gray, and boring. Dante's Hell in *The Divine Comedy* offers a marvelous variety of tortures, humiliations, agony, and extremes of heat and cold. The Khmer Hell of a millennium ago, as shown in a temple in Angkor Wat, teases a glutton by surrounding him with food but giving him a mouth so tiny that he cannot put anything into it. The primitive faith of ancient Israel promised an eternity of agony; later Hebrew scholars modified the pain by obfuscating descriptions of conditions in the Jewish Hell.

Although many men, women, and children have claimed to see God, or to receive personal messages from Him or Her, there is no consensus about God's appearance or personality. The tendency among human beings who describe God has been predominantly anthropomorphic.

There is, however, widespread agreement about the leisureliness of God's responses to human requests. An old Jewish proverb says, "God is an honest payer—but a slow one." Tolstoy named one of his short stories "God Sees the Truth But Waits." Even the ancient Greeks noticed that divine justice often takes its time, as a couplet from *The Greek Anthology* states:

> The mills of the gods grind slow, But they grind exceeding small.

It is not surprising that several poets have written about heaven from the perspectives of animals. Dogs, pigs, cats, and sea-otters have described, through their human amanuenses, the kinds of heaven animals envision. Like the abodes of human beings, these paradises emphasize the physical pleasures animals enjoy during their earthly sojourn.

Rupert Brooke described in detail the kind of heaven the normal fish expects to inhabit:

> Fish say, they have their Stream and Pond;
> But is there anything Beyond?
> This life cannot be all, they swear,
> For how unpleasant, if it were! . . .
>
> And there (they trust) there swimmeth
> One Who swam ere rivers were begun,
> Immense, of fishy form and mind,
> Squamous, omnipotent, and kind;
> And under that Almighty Fin,
> The littlest fish may enter in. . . .

Animals might cite the fact that in the past many creatures were worshipped by human beings. The cat in ancient Egypt, the cow in India, totem animals all over the world make a strong case for equality of animals in that great big space in the sky occupied by postgraduate souls.

One might think that the proliferation of satellites in recent years offers convincing proof that wherever heaven may be, it is not in the atmosphere above us. Still, clergymen giving invocations and public prayers tend to look upward as they address God, obviously assuming that the message will reach its destination faster than if the speaker looked downward.

Human beings sometimes wonder how God keeps track of the millions of prayers that are addressed heavenward, every day and every night. Now that computers perform remarkable feats of record-keeping, the celestial problem may have been facilitated. It is possible, of course, that the IBM existed in heaven, in Platonic form, from the beginning of time. And it is conceivable that the job of the angel who records prayers consists solely of that activity: recording prayers. He may not be required to reply to the prayers, or to inform God about them; like any other bureaucrat in Washington or Moscow he may be carrying out his orders literally. Although every prayer may be recorded, it is possible that none is acted upon.

But this pessimistic idea has never been popular. All over the world people want a response, or the promise of eventual reward. As Mercea Eliade observed: "It is a striking fact that, of all our modern European spirituality, two things alone really interest the non-European worlds: Christianity and Communism. Both of these, in different ways and upon clearly opposed grounds, are soteriologies—doctrines of salvation."[5]

Sports teams often ask for God's help before contests, and some major league baseball players cross themselves every time they come to bat. Why God should help one team rather than another, or one player more than another, is puzzling. It is hard for a detached observer to believe that God is a fanatical sports fan.

People in trouble have always prayed for help. Primitive men and women appealed to spirits, or the sun or moon, or the souls of their ancestors. It is understandable that human beings today, when desperate, also turn for help anywhere they imagine they can get it. A person who usually accepts the scientific explanation of how the universe functions suddenly asks supernatural forces to disrupt the working of natural laws in order to benefit the petitioner. Thus in 1950 the clergymen of New York prayed for rain, as did religious leaders in Texas and elsewhere in other years. Cardinal Spellman once asked all New York Catholics to pray for an end to the polio epidemic.

Hypocrisy in religion appears in many other ways. When someone says that prayer saved him or her in a dangerous situation, people give God credit for the rescue. But when thousands of people perish, in spite of their frenzied prayers, no one blames God for failing to save them. At university convocations in the United States the assigned minister asks for God's participation in the activities of that specific institution. And at Ivy League commencements, God regularly responds to official requests by withholding stormy weather until after the ceremony is concluded.

146

In his study of ritual practices Bocock wrote: "A highly divisive issue during the Reformation concerned prayers for the dead. The Roman Catholic notion of purgatory . . . [resulted in] many corrupt practices around this doctrine, such as the sale of indulgences that enabled the purchaser to buy himself out of so many days, or years, in purgatory."[6]

A fundamentalist congressman from Florida, in a speech to his constituents while he was seeking reelection, deplored the omission of a prayer at the signing of the United Nations Charter: "The history of the UN might have been different had divine guidance been invoked upon the proceedings there." The congressman made no reference to thousands of organizations that began with a prayer and failed abysmally.

There have always been skeptics. In the first century Pliny wrote: "It is ridiculous to suppose that the great head of things, whatever it be, pays any regard to human affairs." Eighteen hundred years later Renan prayed: "O Lord—if there is a Lord, save my soul—if I have a soul."

Prayer has always appealed to wits as an object of satire. Ambrose Bierce, for instance, gave this definition: "Pray, v. To ask that the laws of the universe be annulled in behalf of a single practitioner, confessedly unworthy." Turgenev agreed: "Whatever a man prays for, he prays for a miracle. Every prayer reduces itself to this: 'Great God, grant that two times two be not four.'"

In every country there are jokes directed against that country's religions, and the more dominant the religion is, the more jokes there are that imply criticism of that religion. Hindu, Buddhist, and Confucianist countries are full of material, ancient and modern, that ridicules avaricious, wanton, and deceiving members of the clergy.

Satirists express their opinions in pungent terms. For instance, H. L. Mencken defined church as "A place where men who have never been to heaven talk about it to people who will never get there." To balance this opinion, there is the witticism by Maury White: "Atheist: a man with no invisible means of support."

Humor at the expense of religion is not limited to the Western world. An eighteenth-century Chinese writer, Yuan Mei, expressed his opinion of divinity in a poem that Herbert A. Giles translated under the title "A Scoffer":

> I've ever thought it passing odd
> How all men reverence some God,
> And wear their lives out for his sake
> And bow their heads until they ache.
> 'Tis clear to me the Gods are made
> Of the same stuff as wind or shade. . . .
> Ah, if they came to every caller,
> I'd be the very loudest bawler.

A Unitarian minister in Minneapolis said recently, "It is much easier to be born again than to grow up." And Herb Caen, the San Francisco columnist, wrote, "The trouble with born-again Christians is that they are an even bigger pain the second time around." Nieztsche was more vehement: "After coming in contact with a religious man, I always feel that I must wash my hands."

Sydney Smith, having spent his life as a popular and respected clergyman, concluded, "There is not the least use in preaching unless you chance to catch them ill." Smith also wrote: "The observances of the church concerning fasts and feasts are tolerably well kept on the whole, since the rich keep the feasts and the poor keep the fasts."

Smith was well qualified to speak on the Anglican clergy:

> It is vain to talk of the good character of bishops. Bishops are men . . . subject to the infirmities of old age, like other men; and in the decay of strength and understanding, will be governed as other men are, by daughters and wives. . . . I have seen wife bishops, daughter bishops, butler bishops, and even cook and housekeeper bishops.[7]

Mencken wrote, "An actor jumps from the couch to the altar almost as fast as the Puritan runs from the altar to the couch." In Ben Franklin's amusing anecdote a missionary tells

American Indians about Adam and Eve's un-happy experience with the apple in the Garden of Eden. The Indians agree: "You are right. They should not eat apples. It is better to make apple cider."

An ancient Japanese proverb says, "It is usu-ally the wickedest man who knows the nearest path to the shrine." Commenting on celestial criteria of aesthetics Voltaire wrote, "God has a decided taste for vocal music, provided it is gloomy and melancholy enough."[8]

With a change in the name of the Holy Book, Ambrose Bierce's definition of a Christian ap-plies to any religionist: "Christian, n. One who believes that the New Testament is a divinely inspired book admirably suited to the spiritual needs of his neighbor."[9]

Humorists sometimes lack reverence when they discuss theology, as when A. E. Housman wrote:

> And malt does more than Milton can
> To justify God's ways to man.

Thomas Hardy suggested that God may be asleep. Japanese worshippers, assuming that the god of the temple they are approaching may not be paying attention, clap their hands several times to arouse him. At Shinto weddings the priest bangs on a metal gong for a long time, to make sure that the god is awake and participat-ing in the expensive ceremony.

Vincent Van Gogh leaned over backward in trying to be fair: "I believe more and more that one should not judge God on the basis of this world. It's a sketch of his that didn't come off." And Heinrich Heine, in a letter he wrote in 1850, said: "I lie doubled up, in pain night and day, and though I believe in God I sometimes do not believe in a good God."[10] And R.H. Blyth, an Englishman who spent his adult life teaching in Japan, concluded, "God watches our sufferings, not with pity, not with pleasure, but with interest." How Professor Blyth gathered this information is not revealed.

To an extraterrestrial visitor many procedures in the religions of Earthlings would appear contradictory—and often hypocritical. In America, for example, there are many small religious sects whose members contribute generously to the welfare of their charismatic leaders. In 1936, Frank Buchman, head of the Moral Rearmament Movement, when criticized for luxurious living in the heart of the depression, replied, "Isn't God a millionaire?" More recently, Herbert W. Armstrong, founder of the Worldwide Church of God, excommunicated his son, Garner Ted. The younger Armstrong had founded a similar church of his own. In a letter to his followers, who contributed 65 million dollars a year, Father Armstrong fulminated: "This Garner Ted Armstrong Church has now started a campaign to draw away whatever sheep and shepherds he can entice to follow him—to follow a man instead of a Living God."

The most popular evangelist in America, Billy Graham, told an audience in Copenhagen:

> I have found the best approach is not the intellectual approach, but the most simple way. I have been told that the average American has the intelligence of a twelve-year-old boy. I have found out that was true. We must speak to the people in a language they understand.

Keeping up with electronic times, Christian ministers and evangelists have learned to make effective use of radio and television. Most of these saintly evangelists ask their listeners and viewers to pray that God bless the program and insure its continuance on the air by means of financial contributions from the audience. TV evangelist Jim Baker explained that he and his wife Tammy required a million-dollar salary, several mansions to live in, an air-conditioned dog house, and similar luxuries in order to better serve the members of the public who sent in money for supporting overseas missions.

When Paul Gaugin arrived in Tahiti he found "Missionaries, Protestant and Catholic, grotesquely fighting among themselves for the souls of the natives whose beautiful bodies they ... tried to conceal."[11] A news story in the United States told of a five-year-old minister who performs marriage ceremonies, puts money in his piggy-bank, and rides a toy truck around his Christmas tree. Another story concerns a fifteen-year-old evangelist who claims he spent five hours in Heaven. What made the story newsworthy was not the boy's extraordinary visit but the arrest of his manager for mishandling funds the boy was earning in frequent appearances before large audiences.

Some religions oppose contraception, planned parenthood, and population control on the grounds that every human birth is sacred. It is somewhat difficult to see God's involvement in the birth of infants whose parents participate in baby-derbies in Italy and Canada. Nor would an unbiased observer hold God responsible for faulty contraceptives.

Buddha insisted that he was a human being, not a god; that neither pictures nor sculptures of him should be made; and that he should not be worshipped. But anyone who lives in a country like Sri Lanka can see thousands of figures prostrating themselves daily before images of the Buddha and praying for his help. Islam teaches that no image of Muhammad should be made, and Muslims are very vigorous in objecting to violations of this precept. In Indonesia the Minister for Religious Affairs announced a ban on Volume 17 of the *Funk and Wagnall's Encyclopedia*. The minister explained that a picture of the prophet Muhammad holding a sword in one hand and the Koran in the other gave the totally false impression that Islam had spread by force.

Some years ago, when Virginia Mayo was a popular movie star, the Rev. A. J. Long, a London priest, wrote in the church paper: "Virginia Mayo is the most striking proof of God's existence. Why not? The beauty of woman is a revelation of God to man." Granted that beautiful women make life more pleasant, the Reverend Long avoided the annoying corollary: Does the presence of ugly women prove the existence of the Devil? It is a similar inconsistency on the part of religious apologists that creates a dilemma. Orthodox theologians argue that the orderliness of life on earth is proof of God's existence. But they reject the argument that the enormous amount of disorder on earth is proof of the non-existence of God.

Religions have found ingenious methods of helping worshippers expiate their sins. On Yom Kippur, the annual Day of Atonement, Orthodox Jews are permitted to throw the year's accumulated sins into a conveniently located body of water. On any day of the year, Roman Catholics can confess to a priest and be assigned a penance. Primitive tribes had annual rites of purification, some by water and some by fire. Certain tribes of American Indians periodically made a bonfire of all their possessions and then moved on. And on Taiwan many people still practice the ancient custom of throwing paper into fire to atone for past sins and to request supernatural assistance in the future.

Hypocrisy in religion is definitely not limited to the Western world. In ancient Indian tales, many of them written before the Current Era, religion comes in for a good deal of ridicule. A startling number of Hindu priests and monks in these stories exhibit vanity, pomposity, and an unclerical interest in sex. The famous Indian jester, Tenali Rama, frequently exposed the greed and venality of the Hindu priests he met. And a character in the *Panchatantra* warns that the surest way to get to Hell is to become a priest.

"With money you can move the gods," says an ancient Chinese proverb. The discrepancy between the aspirations of religion and the imperfections of human beings also appears often in Japanese literature. In Saikaku's *This Scheming World* all the people attending a temple for New Year's Eve services admit that they came for non-religious purposes. Saikaku also describes the life of a priest's mistress, concealed in the temple. In *Hizakurige,* a priest sells pictures of the goddess Kwannon that he claims will cure all diseases. In the same book, the chief priest of a large temple entertains and flatters two rogues who, he thinks, have won a lottery; as soon as he discovers his mistake he has them thrown out. Dull sermons, nymphomaniac nuns, lecherous priests, all have provided material for Oriental scoffers.

In 1984 the Tokyo regional taxation bureau accused some Buddhist priests of ignoring the law: one priest used unreported income to maintain two mistresses; another gave his wife an untaxed $95,000 mink coat and a $45,000 diamond ring. Other Buddhist priests in Japan, the tax bureau claimed, had been concealing the income from the lucrative ecclesiastic function of writing for clients posthumous names that ensure dead Japanese Buddhists passage to the next world. The fee for an ordinary *kaimyo* may cost $1,000; more extravagant posthumous names have sold for a million dollars.

The naming of gods by different cultures has always presented a problem. Theologians may pretend that all monotheists are really worshipping the same god, but the man in the street does not believe that Jehovah, Allah, Brahma, and Mr. Moon are the same deity.

Nor is it a new belief that those who belong to other religions are worshipping false gods. Communism became a surrogate for the Orthodox Church in Russia and appropriated many of the Church's psychological appurtenances. Other powerful emotional movements in other countries utilize the repressed fanaticism of individuals for their own purposes. In many people's lives the worship of money, the state, or of an absurd delusion, transcends the worship of their nominal god. Many people go through stages, worshipping first the god they were taught to worship, then Reason or Marx or Freud or the Chicago Cubs, eventually finding none of these completely satisfactory.

There is no denying that the mechanical element has already cheapened the pristine purity of traditional worship. In Muslim mosques loud-speakers magnify the muezzin's call to prayer. Christian drive-in services draw large crowds of worshippers who had been urged, in large ads, to come as they are. A chaplain in the Aleutian Islands during World War Two kept complaining about poorly connected loud-speakers and incorrectly printed programs; he was less concerned with the quality of his sermons. The screaming evangelists who conduct radio revival services ignore the possibility that God deserves greater dignity than they offer Him. And some members of liberal congregations—Christian and Jewish—attend services for the sole purpose of having a place where their children can go to Sunday School.

It is worth considering what happened to the discarded gods of the past. Where are Zeus, Hera, Dionysus, Aphrodite, and their colleagues? Where are Odin, Thor, and Freya of the ancient Scandinavians? Where have the pre-Muslim gods of Southeast Asia gone? Are they still around, with diminished powers, drawing their Social Security checks augmented by cost-of-living raises? If the existence of worshippers proves the existence of gods, does the disappearance of worshippers terminate the gods? After the nuclear war will the God of the Christians, Jews, and Muslims cease to exist?

. . . .

For many people religion is essentially the transformation of ethics and metaphysics into simple, easily understandable proverbs. The average person wants a slogan to repeat, an aphorism to look at. He or she may not have the slightest intention of doing what the maxim recommends. The mere act of looking at a bromide or repeating a cliché is sufficient to confer upon most people a pleasurable feeling, almost as satisfying as taking action might have done. Bernard Shaw was aware of perverted values when he wrote, in the Preface to *Androcles and the Lion:*

> The great danger of conversion in all ages has been that when the religion of the high mind is offered to the low mind, the lower mind, feeling its fascination without understanding it, and being incapable of rising to it, drags it down to its level by degrading it. . . . The conversion of a Savage to

> Christianity is the conversion of Christian-
> ity to savagery.

It would be entertaining to watch a Zulu witchdoctor debate points of doctrine with a Christian, Jewish, or Muslim theologian. Since there is no more scientific evidence to support the supernatural claims of the major religions than there is to defend African superstition, an extraterrestrial spectator might observe such a dispute with considerable amusement. The spectator could not help but be struck by the irony of modern theology: subtle, intellectual, learned—and untenable.

A familiar metaphor makes all of us passengers on a ship sailing perilous seas. To some of the travelers questions occur: Is there a captain aboard? If there is, does he know what he is doing? It is natural for human beings to ask these questions, and it is hypocritical to pretend that such queries are blasphemous. Tennyson wrote:

> There lives more faith in honest doubt,
> Believe me, than in half the creeds.

Attitudes toward deities vary from total reverence at one extreme to the kind of quid-pro-quo relationship that the Japanese exhibit. But in every religion, if worshippers were honest they would admit that they want God to be answerable to them, not them to be accountable to God. Harry Emerson Fosdick once wrote: "God is not a cosmic bell-boy for whom we can press a button to get things." But most people would like God to be a cosmic bell-boy, on call twenty-four hours a day.

Hypocrisy affects the processes of reasoning when people apply them to religion. The same scientists who vigorously reject the idea that scientific truth can be attained by majority vote somehow convince themselves that religious truth has been attained because a majority of their neighbors share it. The same scientists who demand rigid, demonstrable, and repeatable data in their professional work are willing to accept preposterous hypotheses in their religion. The Lord knows, if He has been following this inquiry at all, that the road to science is not the road to fundamentalist religions.

There is no denying the average person's need for religion or a substitute for religion. To the limited extent of their reliability, Gallup's Polls claim that approximately 95% of the people living in the United States believe in God, and 78% believe in immortality. Surveys in France reveal much lower figures, and Russian sociologists said that very few of their people indulged in these capitalistic delusions.

Many Christians have wondered how Jesus would feel about Christianity if He returned to earth. Dostoevsky visualized the Inquisitor of Spain putting Jesus in prison because of the conflicts between His teachings and the actions of the institutionalized church. But Catholics are not the only Christians who refuse to accept poverty or turn the other cheek. A. Powell Davies, a Unitarian minister, in a sermon called "The Danger of Preaching from the Bible," said that any minister who urged his congregation to practice the teachings of the Sermon on the Mount would lose his congregation quickly. The Reverend Sydney Smith agreed: "When an argument taken from real life, and the actual conditions of the world, is brought among the shadowy discussions of Ecclesiastics, it always occasions terror and dismay."[12]

In the eighteenth century an anonymous Chinese poet expressed his opinion:

> You asked me why I greet the priest
> But not his God;
> The God sits mute, the man at least
> Returns my nod.
>
> trans., Herbert A. Giles

At the end of a commentary on hypocrisy in religion, it is worth repeating: the hypocrisy lies not in the noble ideals that every major religion professes to believe, but in the camouflaged failure of clergy and congregations to practice those ideals.

Twelve

Law, Business, and Other Deceptions

*There's a lot of hypocrisy and so forth in political
life. It's necessary in order to get into office and
in order to retain office.*
— *Richard Nixon*

In many ways the lawyer is an appropriate
example of hypocrisy in civilized society. He or
she is trained to defend the innocent and the
guilty, the exploited and the exploiter, the government and the law-breaker, the criminal and
his victim. Ironically, the noble concept that everyone is innocent until proven guilty has been
perverted by lawyers into the ignoble practice
of proving that the guilty person is innocent. In

the legal profession hypocrisy is not only pervasive; it is indispensable.

There is an absurd anomaly in the Anglo-Saxon tradition: although witnesses and litigants are compelled to swear that they will tell the truth and nothing but the truth, lawyers are permitted to lie. Lawyers for the defense are expected to pretend that their clients are always innocent; prosecutors are required to pretend that all accused persons are guilty.

Another absurdity results from good intentions; in the United States, before a conversation can be recorded electronically, all the participants must agree to permit the recording. Since few criminals are eager to confess on tape that they have committed crimes, irrefutable evidence on electronic recordings is often ruled inadmissible in court. So murderers who admitted killings on tape have gone free. And a man who told a policeman where he buried the body of a little girl he had killed was permitted to have that confession thrown out of court because the policeman had not properly cautioned him.

A defense lawyer in Colorado persuaded a judge, and two subsequent Appellate Courts, that his client's confession should be thrown out because the defendant had been coerced. The coercion, the lawyer explained, had been committed not by the police but by God, who disturbed the murderer's conscience so much that he confessed. The Supreme Court eventually restored sanity by over-ruling the Appellate Court.

Again and again we see the unreliability of appearances. In thousands of law cases honest witnesses describe the same event in contradictory terms. In numerous law cases honest witnesses identify innocent persons as guilty, and fail to identify the guilty. Erie Stanley Gardner, a lawyer before he became a writer of popular detective stories, once wrote an article listing twelve cases of misidentification that he had observed. There is no litmus paper test or divining rod that infallibly reveals the truth.

An enormous area of controversy is opened when one asks: Is legal truth actual truth? In 1985, when an American lawyer, Herbert Young, made a serious statement about the nature of legal justice, a newspaper printed his definition under the title *Quips:* "Justice is relative. It is different in Peoria and Paris, in Long Beach and Leningrad. It was different twenty years ago, and it will be different twenty years hence. What we call justice is a momentary consensus." Attorney Young was quite right. In the United States, every time the Supreme Court reverses an earlier ruling, what was true becomes untrue and what was erroneous becomes correct. When the ruler or the governing body of a nation makes new laws, or repeals old ones, "truth" changes. Drinking hard liquor in the United States was illegal from 1920 to 1932, but legal before and after that in most states. Women could not vote for certain offices before 1920 but could vote for them after that. An American who was found guilty of murder can be legally executed in some states, but can only be sentenced to imprisonment in others.

The strict law of the Koran requires the cutting off of thieves' hands and the public execution of adulterers. Hammurabi's Code, 4,000 years ago in Babylonia, was based on a simplistic reciprocity: an eye for an eye, a cow for a cow, a life for a life. Laws in modern Holland are considerably more lenient. But there is no law created by human beings that is universally accepted or permanently applied.

The world of the courtroom is a fantastic realm, operating outside the normal society of human beings. In the legal world common sense is often irrelevant, restrictions on ordinary human communication are artificial, and ridiculous precedent transcends obvious justice. An innocent person who has been declared guilty becomes guilty, as far as the law is concerned. If undeniable proof of guilt has been obtained by a technical violation of an existing, and often temporary, legal requirement, the criminal, whether a petty thief or a murderer, must be permitted to go free in the United States. But in some other countries the law assumes that a person is guilty until innocence is proved.

Charles Dickens has a character in the *Pickwick Papers* say, "If the law supposes that, the law is an ass, a idiot." In *The Deserted Village* Oliver Goldsmith wrote, "Laws grind the poor, and rich men rule the law." It has been long observed that in its infinite wisdom the law forbids both the poor and the rich to sleep under bridges. That experienced mayor, Montaigne, wrote: "I believe that it would be better for us to have no laws at all than to have them in so prodigious numbers as we have." Solon said that "laws were like cobwebs—if any trifling or powerless thing fell into them, they held it fast; while if it were something weightier, it broke through them and was off." Aristotle was not an absolutist: "Even when laws have been written down, they ought not always to remain unaltered." And Tennyson, in "Aylmer's Field," speaks of "the lawless science of our law, That codeless myriad of precedent, That wilderness of single instances."

Thoreau, in "Civil Disobedience," solved the conflict between moral law and civil law by declaring, "I am a human being first, and a citizen second," and went to jail for a night because he disobeyed a civil law. But the New Testament recommends the opposite procedure: "Render therefore unto Caesar the things that are Caesar's, and render unto God the things that are God's." Montaigne made a subtle point when he observed, "Our law has, they say, legitimate fictions on which it founds the truth of its justice."

The peculiarities of the law, apart from the fact that it keeps changing, are intriguing. In American law, for example, a "letter itself—the tangible piece of paper—becomes the physical property of the person who receives it. But the 'literary rights' in the letter—the right to publish it—remain with the author."[1] Certain statements cannot be made in court in the form of declarative sentences but can be expressed as questions. A remark made aloud in court can be expunged from the record by the judge, creating the legal fiction that the remark was never made. When two people have participated in a private dialogue, and both claim under oath to have made contradictory statements, how does a judge determine who is committing perjury? The decision of a judge is valid until it is overruled by an appellate court and becomes valid again when a high court overrules the appellate court.

Several states in the United States have laws making life-imprisonment mandatory for bank robbers under certain conditions; there is no such punishment for murderers. So property seems to be more important to the law than life.

The ancient Chinese knew what they were talking about when they coined the proverb "Win your law-suit and lose your money." In the fourteenth century a Persian writer named Obaid of Zakan defined "lawyer" as "One who proves that right is wrong." His medieval compatriot, Do-Pyazah, coined this definition: "Lawyer. One ready to tell any lie."

There is a story about a man who stood up in court and shouted, "Judge, I demand justice." The judge looked at him for a long time and then said, "What have I to do with justice? This is a court of law."

. . . .

According to a satiric proverb, "In politics there are no permanent friends or enemies." In relationships between nations there are no permanent friends or enemies, only temporarily useful allies or antagonists. Several countries who fought on one side in World War One chose the other side in World War Two and are available for advantageous partnership on either side in World War Three. European nations express noble principles, but they often refuse to take steps against terrorism that is practiced by their trading partners, or to object to the violation of civil rights by powerful neighbors. The European nations that beg for American military cooperation when the Europeans need help, often refuse to aid the Americans in their conflicts.

Capitalistic countries reject the Marxist dictum
of economic determinism, but they make economic determinism the basis of their foreign
policy. Governments preach that corruption
must be exposed, but the persons who expose
governmental corruption are often punished
severely. And the United States under President
Reagan provided military equipment to terror-
ist Iran while it urged its NATO allies to have
no dealings with that country.

Scholars have shown that the Liberal of
nineteenth-century England expressed the same
ideas as does the twentieth-century Conservative. Norman Thomas's Socialist platform of the
1930s was almost completely adopted by non-
Socialist America a half-century later.

The Chinese long ago accepted a hypocritical fact of political life when they coined the
proverb "The conquerors are kings, the losers
are bandits." The Japanese put it this way: "If a
man steals gold he is put in prison; if he steals a
land, he is made a king." An ancient Persian
witticism says, "Fool. An official who is honest." And that experienced politician, Edmund
Burke, remarked, "It is a general public error to
imagine the loudest complainer for the public
to be the most anxious for its welfare."

Richard Nixon stated publicly that a president is not always "lying in an immoral sense"
when he says something he doesn't believe.

"You have to dissemble, you have to recognize that you can't say what you think about an individual because you may have to use him . . . in the future. . . . There's a lot of hypocrisy and so forth in political life. It's necessary in order to get into office and in order to retain office," explained Mr. Nixon. The witticism, "An ambassador is a man sent abroad to lie for his country" is inaccurate only to the extent that sometimes an ambassador is a woman sent abroad to lie for her country. It is not surprising that a great many people refuse to believe anything a politician says and suspect that the term "honest government" is an oxymoron.

Even that venerable oracle of liberalism, *The New Republic,* admitted in its issue of December 8, 1986: "It's true than in international diplomacy, as in personal relations, some hypocrisy is essential." And a book on manners for young diplomats, issued by the British Foreign Office, advised its readers to cultivate acquaintances at funerals, a good place for convulsive handshakes and a chance to offer a lift home. The young diplomat was also encouraged to talk to bores and play bridge with important old women.

Perhaps the most repulsive example of political hypocrisy in the twentieth century was the pretense of Soviet Russia that it represented freedom and democracy. Russian leaders smugly made these claims while their soldiers occupied Poland, Hungary, East Germany, and Czechoslovakia. Russian propagandists blandly ignored walls Communists built to prevent dissatisfied citizens from leaving. And Russian functionaries determined policy in countries that they occupied. The hypocrisy lies not in the tyranny and exploitation—imperialist nations have always brutalized and cheated their victims—but in the sanctimonious pretense that a police state becomes a free state when it is administered by communists. Hypocrisy was not amusing when it pretended that the overwhelming majorities in Eastern European countries who hated the Russians did so because they had been misled by capitalist propaganda.

It is not surprising that in one Czechoslovakian joke, an Englishman comes out of a bar late at night and looks for a taxi to drive him to his hotel. Seeing a cab he signals to the driver and asks, "Are you free?" "No," says the cabby sadly, "I am a Czech."

In another joke, the Russian occupation forces were ordered to fraternize with the populace. A Russian soldier tells a Czech, "You must call me Comrade or Brother." The Czech replies, "I will call you Brother." "That's very nice," says the Russian. "Why?" And the Czech explains, "I can choose my comrades."

The hypocrisy of Communist rule in Poland was exposed by a number of witty Poles. In one joke a man named Kowalski decided to solve his financial problems by getting sent to jail. He went to an important Party meeting and yelled, "You damned Reds! You are filthy liars! You don't know anything about ruling the country. We all hate you!" But nothing happened, and after the meeting the secretary went up to Kowalski and said, "Man, you must be careful. Do you know what would happen to you if there was one real Communist among us?"

A brilliant Polish satirist, Stanislaw Lec, coined the following epigrams:

> The constitution of a country should not violate the constitutions of its citizens.
> In a war of ideas, it is people who get killed.
> Is it progress if a cannibal uses knife and fork?

In Yugoslavia clever satirists also ridiculed Communist hypocrisy. Branco Crncevic wrote: "Men are equal but wages are different." And: "Everything can be heard but not everything can be said." Also: "The revolution does not devour its children, but the grownups better be careful."

Another Yugoslavian writer, Zarko Petan, added a few relevant comments: "Big injustices look smaller from a high position." "A political line is a straight one that turns left or right as the need arises." And: "It's surprising that with us the only healthy currency comes from diseased countries."

Marxist countries, of course, have no monopoly on political hypocrisy. Every other form of government, in the East and in the West, now and in the past, has found hypocrisy an indispensable ingredient of governance. A century ago Republican politician Simon Cameron said: "An honest politician is one who, when he is bought, stays bought."

In 1962, when Prime Minister Macmillan fired a third of his cabinet to give the Tory Party a new image, Liberal M.P. Jeremy Thorpe said, "Greater love hath no man than this, that he lay down his friends for his life." United States Senator Anselm of Mississippi observed, "The basic principle that will ultimately get the Republican Party together is the cohesive power of public plunder."

Unexpected truth is often enlightening, as in Republican Speaker of the House Thomas Reed's reply to a Democratic member who asked, "What becomes of the rights of the minority?" Reed said, "The right of the minority is to draw its salaries, and its function is to make a quorum." Adlai Stevenson described Richard Nixon as "the kind of politician who would cut down a redwood tree, then mount the stump for a speech on conservation." On another occasion Stevenson said, "A politician is a statesman who approaches every question with an open mouth."

A classic exposé of political hypocrisy occurred in Paris during the Revolution of 1848. Amid the confusion of the mobs at the barricades, Leftist Liberal Ledru-Rollin announced, " I've got to follow them. I am their leader."

When small countries are at war with one another, large countries happily provide munitions to both sides, indiscriminately. It has happened in South America, Africa, Asia, and in the Middle East. The war between Iran and Iraq (both Muslim countries) that began in 1980 offers specific examples of international hypocrisy. Iran was at that time a strident enemy of the United States, so a naive observer might expect friends of the U.S. to refrain from helping Iran. Nothing could be further from the truth.

Among the allies of the U.S. selling military materials to Ayatollah Khomeni's brutally fundamentalist, terrorism-sponsoring government were Israel, Spain, Japan, Switzerland, England, West Germany, and South Korea. Spain pretended that the 155mm artillery shells that ended up in Iran had been originally sold to Syria, but Syria did not have any artillery that used 155mm shells. Japan sold what it sanctimoniously called "pleasure boats,"which Iran used for carrying troops through marshland. Switzerland sold Iran jet-training aircraft that they called "civilian airplanes" and recommended the company that would fit them with machine guns. To top off the hypocrisy, the United States itself was secretly selling armaments to Iran at this time.

The ancient Chinese were quite cynical about politics. One of their proverbs says: "An official never flogs the bearer of gifts." Another: "The friendship of officials is as thin as paper." And, finally, "The faults that a man condemns when he is out of office, he commits when in."

. . . .

Business is as guilty of hypocrisy as any other institution. In capitalist societies the businessperson says, "I believe in free enterprise. I want no government interference." But most businesspeople demand that their government protect their particular enterprise with fair-trade laws, or restrictions on foreign competitors, or indirect supports, or direct subsidies "for the good of the nation." The steel industry, shipbuilders, airlines insist that, in this particular case at this particular time, the situation is different and the industry deserves special aid from the government. Farmers contend that they want complete freedom to compete—with the help of government subsidies and guaranteed minimum prices.

In communist countries people say, "I don't believe in private profit," but in every communist country bribes, corruption, and black markets exist. In most instances, in communist and socialist and capitalist countries, in business as in agriculture, education, politics, and religion, the usual rationalization is, "I believe in the general principle, but my case is different."

There is no need to marshal overwhelming evidence to show the hypocrisy of business. The evidence is everywhere. Modern industry depends on "planned obsolescence." Objects are manufactured in such a way that they will begin to deteriorate or fall apart within a specified period, so that the owner will have to buy a new product, whether it is an auto or a razor blade. From the manufacturer's point of view, this is good business. But from an ethical standpoint, deliberately making an inferior product is hypocrisy at best and knavery at worst.

Scholarly articles prove by laborious research what everyone already knows. A relevant example is a recent study by two American professors of "the ethical decision-making process of businessmen." Professor Henry Sims concluded: "If the opportunity for someone to gain something from an unethical decision exists, a helluva lot of people will engage in that unethical decision." Another profound conclusion of the study: "If the individual has something to gain, the probabilities are stronger he will make unethical decisions. When they didn't get the reward, they were a lot more ethical." The researchers made the startling discovery that the more competitive the situation, the greater was the likelihood of unethical behavior. But the threat of criminal punishment "significantly decreased unethical activity." It is encouraging to report that the scholars found one more condition to be true: "Some of the participants in our experiments behaved with perfect ethics even under the most tempting conditions."

Describing a course taught at Cornell University's Graduate School of Business, *Newsweek* wrote: "Cynics might say that modern business and Machiavelli were meant for each other." Machiavelli's sixteenth century handbook for rulers, *The Prince*, was bedside reading for leaders of communist and fascist governments—and of millions of other people all over the world who pretended that they studied it only in order to know what their wicked adversaries might be expected to do. The professor teaching the course defended it: "Most management courses assume that all people are either passive, nice, or stupid. We deal in the reality—that people are also aggressive, self-seeking, and down-right mean." The professor argued that Machiavellian behavior is not necessarily "evil, heartless, and hurtful." No, Machiavelli recommended that when benevolent deeds or decent actions prove useful, it is permissible to act like a virtuous human being, as long as one's behavior is publicized to the proper parties. The students in the class decided that Richard Nixon was an unsatisfactory model not because he behaved badly but because he got caught.

A *reductio ad absurdum* of friendliness is the commercialization of acquaintanceship by Better Brush Parties or Jewelry Gatherings or Neighborhood Fashion Displays, to which people are invited not because they are liked by the hostess but because they are possible customers for a particular product. There is, conceivably, a lack of genuine affection in the Welcome X or Welcome-Y signs temporarily put up by stores near conventions. There is, possibly, sham in billion-dollar corporations expressing on television and radio their warm Christmas greetings to each viewer and listener. These corporations have a deep concern for the welfare, during the New Year, of each member of their audience. It is not surprising that some large institutions hire people whose job is to serve as public scapegoats, to accept the blame for whatever goes wrong, and to pretend to accept the punishment that mollifies dissatisfied customers.

In spite of instructions that forbid such behavior, real estate salespeople misrepresent the property they are selling, automobile salespeople lie about the second-hand cars they are peddling, and the warning *caveat emptor* ("let the buyer beware") is not limited to ancient Rome. When a salesperson praises the dress a woman is examining, or when another clerk recommends the shoes she is trying on, her knowledgeable companion should warn her, "Don't believe a word they tell you. It's their job to sell as much as they can sell." Perhaps that is why the Persian writer Obaid of Zakan coined this definition: "Businessman. One who is not afraid of God."

In the 1930s Gerald K. Smith was one of the most popular bigots in the country, drawing large crowds to his anti-Semitic, anti-Black, anti-Catholic speeches. His headquarters was a building in an Arkansas town. The citizens in that town told an interviewer that they themselves were not prejudiced, but they wholly approved of Smith's operation because it was the largest tourist draw in the state.

Protesting the dumping of foreign steel in the United States, Senator John Heinz of Pennsylvania charged that steel producers in Japan, Korea, and Taiwan "have been forking out subsidies, they have been cutting out competition and knifing American workers, and they have been spooning out platitudes about how they believe in free and fair trade, but they practice absolutely the opposite."

In November 1986, *Fortune* magazine published a long article on the Mafia in the United

States. The writer of the article, Ann Morrison, concluded: "The parallels [of the Mafia] to business organizations and strategies are striking." It is not an accident that Hermes was the Greek god of merchants—and of thieves.

. . . .

The dictionary definition of "advertising" is: "To describe or present (a product, organization, idea, etc.) in some medium or communication in order to induce the public to buy, support, or approve of it."

Advertising is a perfect illustration of the Platonic concept that ideas have reality. It is not products or politicians or religions that advertising conveys; it is *ideas* about products and politicians and religions. The ideas need not be true; for successful advertising, they usually should not be true. Truth coarsens the idyllic image, fact vulgarizes the seductive concept, and logic exposes pretensions. It is only in imagination that an antiperspirant can make one sexually irresistible, a politician can masquerade as a sage, and the supernatural may seem accessible. Advertising is the mass sale of delusions, a process based on hypocrisy.

An Australian aborigine who looked at the advertisements on American television for the first time would have to be warned, "These advertisements are not supposed to be truthful." Familiarity breeds not only contempt but acceptance. Mechanized expressions of good will are regarded as normal: "Thank You for Shopping at Target," says a large sign in a discount store, and the anesthetized customer smiles approvingly. A napkin in a fast-food restaurant bears the slogan, "Thank you" and the diner nods idiotically. A sign in a store says, "Have a Good Day," and the passer-by perks up as if a human being who cared had urged him or her to be happy. We are surrounded by false advertisements and lying endorsements and perjured testimonials, and we are so battered by the sheer mass of communications that we accept the false as true. Repetition transcends veracity. The fact that a statement is made, again and again, eventually outweighs the fact that the statement is not true.

In wartime there is an infuriating quality about ads that brazenly tie the hardships of battle to the virtues of particular products and somehow create the illusion of altruistic endeavor on the part of the manufacturer. For example, "Lucky Strike green has gone to war" was an ad slogan during World War Two.

The ethics of advertising don't seem to have changed much. An old Chinese proverb says "Though we often hear peddlers praise their products, we never hear them call out 'Bitter melon' or 'Thin wine.'"

Sometimes the pretense is amusing, as in fortune cookies, advice from scales on which one has been weighed, and the expressions of good will on plastic containers. In stores and restaurants one is greeted with sham statements of affection. Waiters and waitresses whom one will never see again inquire concerning one's health with the total indifference of programmed robots.

Most advertising is, by any strict test of honesty, hypocritical. Most public relations procedures are, by any strict test of truth, hypocritical. All of these activities involve conscious distortion of the truth, either by claiming virtues that don't exist, or exaggerating achievements, or selecting the few positive aspects among many negative ones. It is true that all social activity requires selection from several possible elements. But the deliberate choice of self-serving material and exclusion of significant negative evidence is dishonest at worst, hypocritical at best.

. . . .

A casual glance at the day's news reveals a continuous stream of hypocrisy. In one example, a U. S. Congressman is arrested for soliciting a police-decoy prostitute; the previous week this congressman had voted to remove Wayne Hays as chairman of a Congressional Committee because Hays was having an affair with his secretary. The congressman had said: "An elected official's private and public standards should be equally high." In another example of somewhat inconsistent behavior, a Nevada house of prostitution was investigated for refusing to accept Black customers. Prostitution is legal in parts of Nevada and the chairman of the state's Equal Rights Commission initiated a charge that the house violated public accommodation laws. The madam was indignant: "This entire matter is ridiculous. A bordello should have a choice in who [sic] they entertain."

In 1968 President Lyndon Johnson flew to Fort Bragg to give a pep talk to an airborne division leaving for Vietnam. Since those soldiers were elsewhere at a farewell beer bust and in no condition or mood for a presidential farewell, the Army provided, as the President's audience, troops who had just returned from Vietnam. After listening in mutinous confusion to the President's platitudes, the men flew off in a large cargo plane; as soon as the President was gone, the cargo plane returned to Fort Bragg.

When Thorstein Veblen was describing the techniques by which individuals in the Western world display their wealth, he coined the term "conspicuous consumption." Rich members of the Kwakiutl tribe used a more direct method: in potlatch ceremonies they demonstrated their wealth by burning large amounts of it. And in eighteenth-century India, when custom occasionally required widows to burn, one woman accepted the ritual for herself but refused to let her jewelry be burned. She too considered property more valuable than human life.

Shortly after World War Two, television stations began to broadcast in the United States. But at that time television sets were too expensive for most people to purchase. So thousands of Americans bought for $2 and proudly displayed on their roofs fake TV antenna that relayed no signal but proved to the neighbors that Thorstein Veblen's theory of conspicuous consumption is still valid.

Americans have no monopoly on vanity: in the past the "ski" ending on Polish names used to indicate a prestigious rank in Poland, where kings often awarded honors to their subjects by permitting them to add "ski" to their name. Many Poles, arriving in the United States as immigrants, added the "ski" to increase their social stature among their new compatriots. Second and third generation Poles tended to drop it.

Social niceties are full of hypocrisy. During the reign of Farouk, the last king of Egypt, gold plates were put on the table on special occasions but removed before the meal was served. Nicholas, the emperor of Montenegro just before World War One, issued his own stamps to enlarge his own stamp collection and awarded himself an inordinate number of large medals.

An American industrialist announced, "What's good for General Motors is good for the country" and was thereupon appointed Secretary of Defense. Labor unions pretend that they are all democratically operated, innocent of all corruption, and motivated only by noble principles. A news story from occupied Berlin after World War Two reported: "The biggest American club in Berlin banned American enlisted men but admitted German frauleins."

If we extend the meaning of "hypocrisy" to include the pretense that one is physically more attractive than she or he really is, an enormous amount of material becomes available. The use of cosmetics was observed and criticized in ancient Egypt and Babylon. The ladies, and some men, of imperial Rome wallowed in the use of beautifying materials, driving Juvenal to fury. (Cosmetics, of course, were not the only objects of Juvenal's satire.)

In seventeenth-century England Robert Burton wrote several passages on the subject of spurious beautification: "Natural beauty is a stronger loadstone of itself . . . but much more when those artificial enticements and provocations of gestures, clothes, jewels, pigments, should be annexed unto it." Also: ". . . those glittering attires, counterfeit colors, headgears, curled hairs, plaited coats, cloaks, gowns, costly stomachers, and all those other accoutrements wherewith our countrywomen counterfeit." Finally: "When you have all done, the greatest provocations of lust are from our apparel; God makes, they say, man shapes."[2]

More than a century later, in 1770, a Bill was introduced in the English Parliament containing the following provisions:

> That all women . . . that shall impose upon, seduce, and betray into matrimony any of His Majesty's subjects by the scents, paints, cosmetic washes, artificial teeth, false hair, Spanish wool, iron stays, hoops, high-heeled shoes, bolstered hips, shall incur the penalty of the Law in force against Witch-craft and like misdemeanors, and that the marriage, upon conviction, shall stand null and void.[3]

The use of artificial stimuli to beauty, or what the user thinks is beauty, is not limited to ancient times or capitalist societies. Green eye-shade was popular with Communist air stew-ardesses, and there was a black market in West-ern cosmetics in Eastern European countries.

An entire industry exists wherein shrewd operators use some form of "inspiration" to defraud the gullible. It is hard to believe that a simple phrase like "accentuate the positive" could be developed into popular books, success-ful seminars, and professional programs. But Emile Coue made millions of Frenchmen, and eventually other Europeans and Americans, walk around saying to themselves, "Every day,

in every way, I am getting better and better."
Dale Carnegie became a millionaire by writing
How to Win Friends and Influence People. Howard
Vincent Peale acquired an enormous audience
by preaching "The Power of Positive Thinking."
Hundreds of people have written self-improve-
ment books that improved the fortunes of the
authors, although they did not do much for the
readers.

Physicians display the Hippocratic oath in
their offices, but private practice offers better
care than socialist medicine; some doctors keep
a closer eye on their investments than on their
patients; and some hospitals in the United States
turn away emergency patients who lack the
proper insurance. In 1936 the Royal Physician
gave King George V of England an injection to
hasten his death so that the story would make
the morning papers.[4]

One ancient Egyptian king had an official
court liar. He would have no trouble finding
employment today.

Thirteen

The Animal Kingdom

*A dignified-looking dog is the first to get onto
the dinner table, when it is not watched by its
master.*
                              —*Korean proverb*

At first glance, the notion that animals can
be hypocritical seems ridiculous. Most people
assume that only human beings are blessed with
the capacity for self-serving duplicity. But hypocrisy is a certain kind of deceit, and there is
overwhelming evidence that animals are deceitful. Whether some of that deception can be
called hypocrisy is worth considering.

Ethologists are uncertain about the limits of
animal faculties. Maurice Burton writes, "Can
animals experience feelings of grief, fear, hate,

love, awe, reverence, and so on? The layman will say, at once, that there is a *prima facie* case for believing they do, but the zoologist is less sure."[1]

And Nobel Laureate Konrad Lorenz says:

> The central nervous system of animals is constructed differently from ours, and the physiological processes in it are also different from what happens in our brain. However . . . we are convinced that animals do have emotions, though we shall never be able to say exactly what those emotions are. My teacher Heinroth . . . used to say, "I regard animals as very emotional people with very little intelligence."[2]

The line between hypocrisy and other forms of deceit is sometimes very thin; undeniably, animals do a great deal of pretending. There is the dissemblance of the stalking animal that pretends that it is not pursuing prey. And there is the dissemblance of the stalked animal pretending that it is not where it is or camouflaged to pretend that it is something different from what it is.

Animals often use trickery for practical purposes. Certain male baboons help each other gain access to females by fighting with rivals. Harvard anthropologist Irven DeVore has no doubts about animal guile. "The animal kingdom is absolutely overrun with examples of deception," he writes. "Every fish; every lizard; every bird that has a crest, a coloration, or any such thing that exaggerates its size—that's deception."[3]

A great many examples of animal trickery that demonstrate that higher animals practice more sophisticated forms of deceit than lower creatures, are cited in a book by Mitchell and Thompson: *Perspectives on Human and Nonhuman Deceit.*

It is not easy to decide whether mere deception or ingenious hypocrisy is practiced by the female firefly *Photinus* when she sends out rhythmic flashes of light that attract males of the same species. "It modifies its signal to mimic the flash patterns of different species of fireflies and thus lures unsuspecting males. Once they are in reach, the female devours them."[4]

The variations of insect trickery are fascinating. For instance, a carnivorous fly, the *Empid,* faces the danger of being devoured by the female before mating. So he presents her with a small fly or an object that he enshrouds with fine silk threads secreted from his legs. While she is unraveling the binding, the mating takes place.[5]

It is fair to ask whether parasitism is exploitation, deception, or arrant hypocrisy. Ants, bees, and wasps practice what Edward O. Wilson calls "temporary social parasitism." Wilson tells us: "Birds having altricial [helpless] young are especially vulnerable to brood parasitism, in which females of other species insert their eggs into the nests and trick the hosts into raising their young."[6] About eighty species of birds indulge in "brood parasitism," including no less than fifty varieties of cuckoos.

The degree to which some parasites achieve their objectives is extraordinary. Whether we should call it incredible deception or extreme hypocrisy is a problem of semantics. But Edward O. Wilson's description of insect duplicity resembles the infiltration of spies in a LeCarre novel.

> As Wheeler said, "Were we to behave in an analogous manner we should live in a truly Alice-in-Wonderland society. We should delight in keeping porcupines, alligators, lobsters, etc. in our homes, insist on their sitting down to the table with us, and feed them so solicitously with spoon victuals that our children would either perish of neglect or grow up as hopeless rhachitics."[7]

A form of pretense that may be considered hypocritical occurs when a creature, animal or human, substitutes one activity for another because of timidity. Konrad Lorenz cites an example in which pretense is an important element. In the rare instances where two close male friends (in this case, ganders) have "deritualized" their relationship by a vicious fight,

> The victor never pursues the vanquished, ... On the contrary, they avoid each other meticulously from thenceforth. ... If by chance they do come near each other, they show the most remarkable behavior that I have

ever seen in animals. . . . The ganders are
embarrassed! . . . They cannot simply walk
away, for any action suggestive of flight is
forbidden by the age-old commandment to
"save face" at any cost.[8]

In his survey of animal behavior, Vance
Packard included several examples of displacement activity: Of two female chimps in a lab,
Lia was clearly the dominant and Nira the submissive animal. The psychologist placed a nut
before them. When Nira's hand had almost
reached the nut, Lia calmly took it. "Dr. Birch
reports that in one such frustrating instance
Nira's behavior was quite human: 'Nira, instead
of protesting or withdrawing her hand, continued her movement, carried her hand up to her
face and scratched.'"[9]

Of all the examples of hypocritical pretense
among animals, in behavior and in appearance,
the most obvious take place in courtship.
Among insects, courtship displays are of four
kinds, appealing to sight, touch, hearing, and
smell.

During the courting season one of the animals (usually the male) looks more colorful and
displays more agility than at any other time. A
masquerade conceals the intrinsic self during
the process preliminary to mating. (Sometimes
the mating is for life.) Nature plays an important role in this deception.

Nature helps animals create false impressions. During the rutting season, a change takes place in the larynx of a red deer so that his voice becomes a loud, challenging roar. He wallows in peaty mud, taking on a dark color that is entirely artificial. "The antlers are now fully grown, the neck is covered with a mane, the scent-glands below the eyes have become fully functional."[10]

Vance Packard, in *Animal I.Q.,* cites additional interesting phenomena. "During the mating season the umbrella bird of Central America begins his booming call that can be heard for miles. As he 'displays' for a female, a sack on his throat, normally obscured by black feathers, begins to swell until it is the size and color of a huge red tomato. As a final touch he has a long tassel hanging from the sack. . . .

> An even more stunning show is put on by the male humming bird. In his sexual flight before an admiring girl friend he goes through foolhardy stunts at 600 miles an hour.[11]

The penguin's courting behavior has long aroused human amusement. He picks up a pebble, waddles up to the object of his affection, and drops the pebble at her feet.

The use of scent as a courting device is almost as common among animals as among human beings. Animals have been found to react to certain chemicals at one thousandth of the concentration at which the human nose can detect them. Catamount not only makes the domestic cat leap and bound in a ridiculous manner but also makes pumas and lions engage in similar behavior. In a large number of mammals, special scent-glands are a prominent feature. They are normally quiescent but become markedly active during the breeding season.[12]

A number of ethologists have observed the pretense of indifference or coyness on the part of courted females. Whether these pretenses can be called hypocritical depends on the observer. The female squirrel, pretending to be shy, runs away from randy males, but she never runs too fast to be caught by one of them. Drummer remarks, "Female wild animals, like humans, display modesty during courtship and play hard-to-get, but will turn to decoy the male should his interest be lured toward some other female."[13]

Konrad Lorenz closely observed the behavior of courting geese: "If the gander does court her, she does not react, for a considerable time, by attitude or gesture. It is only the play of her eyes that tells the male how his courtship is received. . . . As she tries to do this without noticeably turning her head, she has to squint at him out of the corner of her eyes just like a girl flirting."[14]

Burton tries to account for the apparent flirtatiousness of courted females:

> Nobody has yet given a satisfactory explanation of what is a widespread phenomenon . . . the mysterious quality of coyness in the female. . . . There is a seeming indifference of the female to the displays and advances of the male. In many instances it has been amply demonstrated, by her subsequent behavior, that she was not as indifferent as she appeared to what was taking place; rather the reverse. It may be that this coyness provides a necessary delay for the critical moment in her breeding physiology to be reached, in order that correct synchronization in the maturing of the germ-cells of the two partners may be achieved.[15]

Edward Wilson offers a different explanation:

> Pure epigamic display can be envisioned as a contest between salesmanship and sales resistance. . . . The courted sex, usually the female, . . . finds it strongly advantageous to distinguish the really fit from the pretended fit. Consequently, there will be a strong tendency for the courted sex to develop coyness. That is, its responses will be hesitant and cautious in a way that evokes still more displays and makes correct discrimination easier.[16]

The ephemeral display of attractive apparel, by birds and by human beings, is hypocritical, for in these displays the exhibitor is showing color, characteristics, or clothing that he or she does not normally possess. Pragmatic hypocrisy may be recognized here.

The display of bright colors is not the only device feathered creatures use to impress the birds they are courting. Others include singing, dancing, aquabatics, and aerobatics.[17]

Some ethologists see a clear relationship between the courtships of animals and those of human beings. That includes, of course, the element of self-serving pretense—hypocrisy—utilized by both animals and people.

Having seen the enormous variety of devices used in animal courtship we must admit that Nature is deceitful. It provides temporary colors to some animals, temporary musical skills to others, and temporary attractive sexual characteristics to still others. The courted female is induced to make a choice based on ephemeral and often misleading evidence. Whatever useful results the duplicity achieves, it remains duplicity. And whatever the purpose of the fraud, a fraud is continually being perpetrated.

. . . .

In addition to obvious deceptions, parasitism, displacement activities, and misleading courtship displays, there are many other examples of actions by animals that may be labeled hypocritical.

A book by London veterinarian Bruce Fogle describes a number of insidious procedures that are used by pets. In *Games Pets Play: How Not to be Manipulated by Your Pet,* Dr. Fogle draws a parallel between animal behavior and the tricks of human beings discussed by Eric Berne in *Games People Play.* Pets often "dominate through submission," says Fogle, identifying one of many strategies used by domesticated animals. "Humans are programmed for lifelong parenting, and pets don't hesitate to take advantage of that." Pets, he claims, are great observers and great psychologists, "better, in fact, than we are." All of this is calculated to obtain those material rewards and those psychological responses that the animal needs, claims Dr. Fogle.

The actions of a monkey who liked liquor offer an amusing example of pretense: "A sick guenon monkey was once placed on a prescription of spirits. This pleasant medicine was given at set hours and the animal soon developed a liking for it. However, when the creature recovered from its illness, the spirits were discontinued. The monkey showed its unhappiness by putting its hands to its belly and moaning and grimacing as though in direst misery, whenever the hour of its former treatment came around again."[18]

The role of hypocritical deception among chimpanzees is given full recognition by Henry W. Nissen of the Yerkes Laboratories. "Sheer strength," he writes, "plays an important role in determining dominance and leadership, but it is by no means the only factor shaping the pattern of social relations within a group of chimpanzees. Ingenuity, trickery, bribery and guile may become more effective than brute force. Some individuals are very successful in getting others to fight their battles or to assist them in a task requiring cooperation."[19]

Still another example of social deception— or hypocrisy—is cited by Edward Wilson:

> When a *hamadryas* female is placed in a group of *anubis* baboons, she quickly alters her social responses from the *hamadryas* forms to those of her new associates. Within half an hour she starts fleeing from attacking males like an *anubis* female rather than moving toward them. The reverse experiment is even more suggestive. An *anubis* female inserted into a *hamadryas* troop learns within one hour to approach the attacking male, thus conforming to the harem system that characterizes this species as opposed to her own.[20]

The pecking order in animal societies results in many examples of hypocritical behavior. "All social animals are 'status seekers,'" says Konrad Lorenz, "hence there is always particularly high tension between individuals who hold immediately adjoining positions in the ranking order."[21] Lorenz gives an amusing example of a low-ranking female jackdaw who was unexpectedly chosen by the new despot of the colony as his mate: "She used every opportunity to snub former superiors, and she did not stop at gestures of self-importance, as high rankers of long standing nearly always do. No—she always had an active and malicious plan of attack ready at hand. In short, she conducted herself with the utmost vulgarity."[22]

Quoting from a work of fiction provides no scientific evidence whatsoever. And yet it may be refreshing to look at some thoughts of an imaginary dog in Anatole France's "Meditations of Riquet."

> "I am in the center of all things; men, beasts, and things, friendly and unfriendly, are ranged about me."
> "An action for which one has been beaten is a bad action. An action for which one has received food or caresses is a good action."
> "O my master Bergeret.... I adore thee.... I crouch at thy feet; I lick thy hands.... Keep me in thine house and keep out every other dog. And thou, Angelique, the cook, divinity good and great, I fear thee and venerate thee in order that thou may give me much to eat."

There is no denying that animals deceive and pretend. What has not been resolved is how much of this deception and pretense can be called hypocritical behavior.

Fourteen

Universality

Great politeness usually means 'I want something.'
—Chinese proverb

In the folklore of many cultures rationalizing is used as an excuse for failure. Aesop's fox pretends that the grapes he cannot reach are sour. And rationalizing serves to defend indefensible behavior. When Aesop's wolf is getting ready to eat a lamb he explains that he is punishing the lamb for polluting the water in the river. The lamb protests that he had been drinking downstream, but the wolf says, "Well, one of your relatives must have drunk upstream," and then eats the lamb.

Other Aesop fables make oblique or direct reference to hypocrisy. After the council of mice approves a proposal to put a bell around the cat's neck, an old mouse says, "An admirable idea. Who is going to bell the cat?" After the lion and the wild ass have hunted as partners, the lion says, "I will take the first third because I am king of beasts. I will take the second because, as partner, I deserve half. And I will take the third, or you will be very sorry." When the old crab tells her son, "Why do you walk sideways? You should walk straight," the young crab replies, "Show me how, mother, and I will follow your example." Still another fable of Aesop tells us that every man carries two bags, one in front of him and one behind. The bag in front contains his neighbors' faults, the bag behind his own. And that is why, says Aesop, men always see the faults of others, never their own.

Asians are as aware of hypocrisy as is everyone else. In India there is a tendency, stemming perhaps from the knowledge accumulated in three thousand years, to accept hypocrisy as an inescapable fact of life. The *Panchatantra*, for example, a collection of ancient Indian folk tales, is full of hypocritical behavior, especially on the part of women, priests, businessmen, and rulers. China too, a very old civilization, expresses a greater tolerance for hypocrisy than do Western idealists.

Hypocrisy provides the richest single source of Western satire, and hypocrisy pervades the behavior of individuals and institutions in Asian satire. The major objects of derision in the Orient prove to be depressingly similar to those in the West. The panders and parasites in the classic Chinese novel *Golden Lotus* make hypocrisy a way of life. In the Japanese novel *I Am A Cat*, a businessman smokes an imported brand of cigarettes that he cannot afford, admittedly to impress other Japanese businessmen. A Chinese proverb says, "Great politeness usually means 'I want something.'" The Japanese parallel: "When a man offers favors, search for his purpose." India adds: "A kinsman, if he is poor, is an outcast." The Jewish version goes "Rich relatives are close relatives; poor relatives are distant relatives."

Although Burma is a fervently Buddhist country, hypocrisy seems to have sneaked past the noble teachings of Buddha, as the following anecdote shows:

> The newly married girl said to her husband, "Look, who is that ugly woman coming up the stairs?"
> "Shh. Speak softly. That is my aunt."
> "She is so ugly I am not going to speak to her."
> "If you don't, she may not give me the thousand rupees she promised us as a wedding gift."

> The wife to the aunt: "Ah, dear auntie, we
> have been looking forward to your visit for
> a long time. Do sit near me where you can
> be comfortable."

In Sri Lanka Buddhism teaches that killing and dishonesty are forbidden. Some Ceylonese have found ways to evade these injunctions. A man who had "taken Sil" for the day—that is, had vowed to observe the Buddhist precepts, including the one ordaining "do not kill"—saw a poisonous snake near his house. In order to follow the precept and yet have the snake destroyed, he yelled to another man near him, "There's the snake, here's the stick, I have taken Sil."

A four-line poem called a *pantun* is a unique example of Malaysian literature. This *pantun*, translated by A.W. Hamilton, suggests that even in Malaysia hypocrisy has reared its head.

> Where barnacles cling to the fort,
> Come, let us row a fishing snack.
> When priests and scribes in sin are caught,
> What chance for us who learning lack?

The device of looking at the world through the eyes of an animal, for satiric purposes, is used in the Indian *Panchatantra*, the Japanese novel *I Am A Cat*, the Chinese narrative *Monkey*, and of course Aesop's and LaFontaine's *Fables*. What the animals see is a great deal of hypocrisy.

The proverbs of a country express widely held beliefs. When one finds contradictory proverbs, one may suspect that society itself is being hypocritical, by providing the public with what the public would like to have, regardless of the authenticity of the product. If Kenneth Burke was right in calling proverbs "strategies for living," society may be two-faced in offering conflicting strategies. In the Western world, for example, we are given the choice of believing that "absence makes the heart grow fonder" or "out of sight, out of mind." We are also advised, "Look before you leap," but "He who hesitates is lost." Japan offers similar contradictions: "A wife and a pot get better as they get older" and "A wife and a floormat are good when new and fresh."

A great many proverbs all over the world clearly recognize the existence of hypocrisy. An old Ceylonese adage says:" 'It is not that I cannot dance, but the floor is not level,' said the dancer." Another Ceylonese aphorism tells us: "Six months after the death of the mother-in-law, a tear came to the eye of the daughter-in-law." Other Ceylonese proverbs that comment cynically on hypocrisy include:

> If broken by the mother-in-law it is an earthen vessel, if by the daughter-in-law it is a gold vessel.

> It is good to be a Headman, even in Hell.
> The ex-priest atoned for his previous celi-
> bacy by taking two wives.

Some Ceylonese and Burmese proverbs are very similar. "One's own fault is invisible, those of others apparent," say the Ceylonese. The Burmese match it with: "In another's, yes, but in his own eye he sees no dirt." But the Burmese have enough of their own proverbs that ridicule hypocrisy:

> He climbs up the pole of the marquee to
> show his almsgiving.
> A full stomach supports moral principles.
> He calls her aunt only when the cucumber
> is ripe.
> His mouth says "Buddha, Buddha," but his
> hand acts differently.
> In Garuda country be a Garuda; in Naga
> country be a Naga.

In Korea too there is humorous comment on hypocrisy, as this proverb demonstrates: "After sobbing and grieving, he asks who is dead."

Hypocrisy was the largest single source of satire in ancient China, and it remains a rich well-spring of humor in China today. A play, *The Day the New Director Came*, ridicules syco-phantic officials. In poetry, hypocritical busi-nessmen were derided by Chten Tzu-ang in the seventh century, hypocritical politicians and philosophers were mocked by Po-Chui in the eighth century, and snobbery and colonialism are debunked by the twentieth-century Yuan Shui-pai. A classic Chinese novel, *The Scholars*, castigates intellectuals, administrators, and parasites who behave hypocritically.

A more recent Chinese novel, *Flowers in the Mirror* by Li Ju-Chen, describes the Country of Two-Faced People, where the face in front smiles while the face in back snarls. In the same book the travelers visit another country, where everyone is accompanied by a cloud that reveals the person's true character; most rich people have a black color (the worst kind). An ancient Chinese essay on "flunkeyism" and a sixteenth-century piece on toadyism by Tsung Ch'en prove that hypocrisy has a long history in China.

Twenty-three centuries ago Lieh-Tzu wrote this anecdote: "There was a man who had lost money and thought that his neighbor's son had stolen it. He looked at the young man and it seemed that his gait was that of a thief, his expression was that of a thief, and all his gestures and movements were like those of a thief. Soon afterwards the man found the money in a bamboo drain pipe. Again he looked at the neighbor's son and neither his movements nor gestures were those of a thief."

Chinese proverbs, the oldest in the world, show great familiarity with hypocrisy. "Money hides a thousand deformities," says one aphorism. "More trees are upright than men," says another. "You cannot tell what is in a man's heart by looking at his face," the Chinese learned a long time ago.

The Chinese share a universal illusion: "The fish that escaped is the big one." Like hosts everywhere, the Chinese have learned: "Long visits bring short compliments." In spite of the tradition of filial devotion, a Chinese proverb states: "There are no loving children at the bedside of long-sick parents." And, long ago, the Chinese found, "Rich doctors don't visit poor patients."

· · · ·

Hypocrisy permeates Japan even more than other societies because the crowded conditions of Japanese life impose a ubiquitous but quite superficial politeness on the people. The courtesy is a very thin veneer. And the gifts and entertainments showered upon guests are often a conditioned form of behavior, not necessarily an expression of affection or respect. The word "no" is rarely used in Japan and "yes" may mean anything from "maybe" to "forget it."

Japanese literature vividly exposes this hypocrisy. Novels like Akatugawa's *Kappa*, Ikku's *Hizakurige*, Saikaku's *This Scheming World*, and Natsume's *I Am A Cat* and *Botchan* show that beneath the smooth surface of Japanese life the same vanity and greed and insecurity promote the same hypocrisy that all other developed civilizations engage in.

A medieval Japanese poem ridicules a man who always managed to find an excuse for eating fish on forbidden days. A modern *senryu* describes a servant being polite to a caller, unaware that he is addressing an insurance salesman. *I Am A Cat* burlesques the cant in letters soliciting funds. And Saikaku satirized homosexual priests, male concubines, and roues who sought out young widows.

In a Japanese joke, the wife is having a difficult delivery. The husband promises the god of Kompira that if his wife has a successful delivery he will donate a copper gate for the god's shrine. "That's nonsense," the wife cries. "You have no money." The husband says: "Quiet. Have the baby quickly while I deceive the god."

The following *senryu* translated by R. H. Blyth make satiric comments on society:

> A visitor came
> So the scolding stopped,
> And was put off for a while.
>
> The wife was sent away;
> But her mother
> Pretends she just left.
>
> Gathering together the ashes,
> Weeping, weeping
> Looking for the gold teeth.
> —Alembo

Some Japanese proverbs about hypocrisy show a striking similarity to the aphorisms of other countries. "No standing in the world without stooping," say the Japanese, reminding us of Jonathan Swift's remark: "Climbing is performed in the same posture with creeping." The Japanese proverb of reassurance, "A fire across the river," reminds us of La Rochefoucauld's cynical epigram: "We all have enough courage to bear up under the troubles of others."

Like several other Asian countries, the Japanese say: "When you buy a vase cheap look for flaws, and when a man offers favors search for a hidden purpose." As in India and China, the Japanese learned: "One cannot tell what passes though the heart of a man by the look on his face."

Unexpected truth leads the Japanese to say, "Virtue carries a lean purse." There is some cynicism in the proverb "Even Yama, the King of Hell, is influenced by money." We have seen elsewhere the refrain: "When victorious, the imperial army; when defeated, a rebel army." And then there is the cynical Japanese maxim: "Deceive, but don't insult, the rich and powerful."

. . . .

From the very beginning of India's three-thousand-year-old culture, hypocrisy has been clearly apparent. In the ancient epic, *Mahabharata,* there are statements accepting hypocrisy as an indispensable requirement for social advancement. India has a reputation in the West as a nation dedicated to spiritual values, but in his description of ancient Indian society J.A.B. Van Buitenen writes: "Kautiliya maintains that of the three principal goals of life—the pursuit of virtue, the pursuit of profit, and the pursuit of love—the second ranks highest."[1]

Among the objects of satire in ancient Indian tales is the serving of luxurious foods to impress guests. In one story a man who had been neglected at a banquet because of his poor clothes leaves the feast, changes his attire, and returns. This time he is treated with respect. "Feed my clothes," he says, "for it is they who are welcome."

The *Panchatantra,* an ancient collection of Indian fables, satirizes deceitful Brahmins and lustful women, the exploitation of wealth and the laziness of servants. In one story, the king of frogs sacrifices all of his subjects to save himself. More hypocrisy is displayed in the folklore of India: A fox lies to a wolf about a tiger, then lies to the tiger about the wolf. A rich man who pretends that he enjoys good music arranges to be signaled when he is to applaud. A man who has found a lost jewel announces the fact but so quietly that no one can hear; his conscience is clear. Another hypocrite refuses to share in a stolen chicken; he takes only the gravy. A king sends his regrets to the family of the man whom he has had executed.

The proverbs of India that deal with hypocrisy are very similar to proverbs elsewhere:

> A friend in need is a friend indeed, Altho
> of different caste,
> The whole world is your eager friend, So
> long as riches last.
> —*Panchatantra*,
> trans., Arthur Ryder

> The cake in the oven is yours; the cake on
> the tray is mine.
> Rare is the man who practices the virtue he
> preaches.
> A thorn sticks in a great man and hundreds
> run to help; a poor man falls down a cliff
> and no one comes near.
> . . . .

In African folk-tales and fables there are many examples of hypocrisy. But it is in the proverbs of different tribes that the recognition of hypocrisy, and warning against deceit, are most succinctly and vividly expressed. In the following proverbs, the range of human duplicity is fairly well covered.

> "Thank you" does not put the pot on the
> fire.
> When you are ill you will promise a goat,
> but when you have recovered a chicken will
> seem sufficient. (Jukun)
> If you have no money to buy wine, then
> you say, "Wine is not good." (Twi)
> When the ape cannot reach the ripe banana,
> he says it is sour. (Bambare)

To the dog that has money men say, "My Lord Dog." (Tunisian)

The fool who owns an ox is seldom recognized as a fool. (Chuene)

He is a near-relative when there are shrimps to be had, but when they are done he is only a distant relative. (Malagasy)

The teeth are smiling, but is the heart?(Congo)

He who seems to be pleading for you may be working against you. (Akofi)

Among many sympathizers, only a few are sincere. (Twi)

In a court of fowls, the cockroach never wins his case. (Congo)

The tongue with which you ask for a loan is different from that with which it is repaid. (Twi)

He who seeks you to borrow does not seek you to repay. (Ganda)

If a doctor is mistaken he leaves by the back of the house. (Ibo)

"May you live and prosper "won't support the wife and family. (Malagasy)

Gratitude is a lotus flower whose leaves soon wither. (Amharic)

If one has many sores, one praises some of them. (Twi)

When one sets a portion for oneself, usually it is not too small. (Ethiopia)

It is easy to become a monk in one's old age. (Ethiopia)

Singing "halleluia" everywhere does not prove piety. (Ethiopia)

Those who are absent are always wrong.
(Congo)

It's a damned unfeeling world, as the scorpion said when he tried to sting the clay pot. (Hausa)

. . . .

During the thirteenth century the great Persian writer Sa'di included this anecdote in the *Gulistan.*

A wise man said to his friend: "What am I to do? I am troubled by the people, many of whom pay me visits. By their coming and going they waste my precious time."
He replied: "Lend something to every one of them who is poor and ask something from every one who is rich, and they will come round no more."

Sa'di also contributed a couple of maxims:

Whoever tells you the faults of your neighbors will also tell others of your defects.
What can an old prostitute do but vow to become chaste, and an expelled policeman not to commit oppression upon men?

Another Persian, Do-Pyazah, added these witticisms:

Widow. A woman in the habit of praising her husband when he is gone.
Faithful Friend. Money.
Liar. A person making frequent use of the expression, "I swear to God it is true."

Persian proverbs reveal the same awareness of hypocrisy as do the aphorisms of other countries:

Himself in disgrace, he gives others free advice.

A friend in time of opulence and a stranger in distress.

He is liberal in etiquette and stingy in gifts.

Soldiers fight, but commanders get the victory.

Free wine is drunk even by the priest.

Trust in God, but tie your camel.

Middle Eastern cultures also have proverbs that recognize hypocrisy in one form or another. "I have a mouth that I feed," say the Arabs, "it must speak what I please."

Other Arab sayings include:

A mouth that prays, a hand that kills.

There are no faults in a thing we want badly.

If they had not dragged me from under him I would have killed him.

The barber learns to shave on the orphan's face.

"All my goods are of silver and gold," says the boaster, "even my copper kettles."

The proverbs of Turkey also comment on hypocrisy:

When a bribe enters the door, law goes out the chimney.

My mother can really weep, other tears are false.

When a rich man falls it is an accident; when the poor man falls he is called a drunk.

On a rainy day many will give water to the chicken.

When the cat cannot reach the meat, he says, "Today is fast-day."

Among the proverbs in the Hebrew Bible are the following:

> Every man is a friend to him that gives gifts. (Prov. 19:6)
>
> Most men will proclaim every one his own goodness; but a faithful man who can find? (Prov. 20:6)
>
> It is naught, it is naught, says the buyer: but when he is gone his way, then he boasts. (Prov. 20:14)
>
> Vanity of vanities, vanity of vanities; all is vanity. (Eccles.)
>
> Jeremiah castigates those who "dissemble in their hearts." (42:20)
>
> The hypocrites' hopes shall perish, says Job. (8:13)

The New Testament reprimands hypocrites:

> When you give alms, sound no trumpet before you, as the hypocrites do in the synagogues and in the streets, that they may be praised by men. (Matt. 6:12)
>
> Mark says that when the Pharisees came to Jesus, "He, knowing their hypocrisy, said to them, 'Why tempt ye me?'" (12:15)
>
> Luke quotes Jesus's warning to the multitude: "Beware ye of the leaven of the Pharisees, which is hypocrisy." (12:1)
>
> Matthew fulminates: "Thou hypocrite, first cast out the beam out of thine own eye" (7:5), and "Even so ye also outwardly appear righteous unto men, but within ye are full of hypocrisy and iniquity." (23:28)

. . . .

With a cynicism rare for him, Spinoza observed, "Those who are believed to be most abject and humble are usually most ambitious and envious." Samuel Johnson told Boswell: "Sir, are you so grossly ignorant of human nature as not to know that a man can be very sincere in good principles without having good practice?" Biologist Edward Wilson lists among "qualities exceptionally pronounced among human societies . . . the capacity to dissimulate."[2] And a popular American comedienne says in her autobiography that she had to adopt the abrasive public persona of "Joan Rivers" in order to "puncture the hypocrisy all around us . . . and strip life down to what it really is."

Clearly, hypocrisy appears in every culture. Clearly, hypocrisy has been characteristic of human behavior for a very long time. And, clearly, the reasons for hypocrisy are similar all over the world.

Conclusion

Some things about hypocrisy are well known. First, it has a very long history. In the scriptures of all great religions and in the literatures of ancient civilizations there are many references to hypocrites. Secondly, hypocrisy is universal. Proverbs, folk tales, and written records all over the world provide ample evidence of hypocritical behavior. Thirdly, hypocrisy is pervasive. It is practiced by individuals and institutions at every level of society.

The hypocrisy of institutions is more reprehensible than the hypocrisy of individuals because it is always calculated, always aware of the institution's actions. Institutions deny guilt when they are guilty, find scapegoats to blame for their failures, and sanctimoniously pretend that their behavior is altruistic and noble when, in reality, it is selfish and greedy. As Pareto explained, institutions rationalize their defects into virtues.

But other aspects of hypocrisy are not so clearly apparent. Though human beings have been closely observing the behavior of animals for millenia, rarely has anyone voiced the suspicion that animals may behave hypocritically. Certainly animals practice deception and pretense. Some insects simulate the scents of other insects, some birds imitate the sounds made by other birds.

We have seen that Nature falsifies the appearance of animals during courting season to make them seem more desirable to prospective mates. Evolution has to encourage mating for continuation of the species. To that end, Nature makes animals look more attractive than they normally do, or more virile than they actually are, or more appealing as mates than they will prove to be.

A surveyor of hypocrisy may reasonably ask whether Nature itself is hypocritical. Though most people are willing to concede that Nature is amoral, to go a step further and consider whether Nature may be hypocritical seems preposterous. And yet, there is a good deal of evidence that, like individuals and institutions, Nature often misrepresents reality in order to achieve a desired result.

Nature has developed, through evolution, a neural system in human beings that filters out disturbing and unflattering messages and facilitates the reception of pleasant and gratifying material. In this process, Nature has created a deceptive condition at that primary level of human activity, the reception of communications from the world outside the organism. This procedure is hypocritical.

Evolution favors responses that allow organisms to survive by any means. One of these means is deception, and hypocrisy is one form of deception. Nature uses evolution to support all activity that helps maintain the continuity of the species. When hypocrisy helps to achieve that end, Nature acts hypocritically. Although it may not be ethical to use hypocrisy, ethics have nothing to do with evolution.

Civilization, on the contrary, is an attempt to bring morality into the conduct of life. Civilization introduces the concepts of kindness, idealism, nobility, charity, honesty. Perhaps, as Freud said, "civilization is repression." But among the impulses that civilization tries to repress are cruelty, greed, selfishness, and brutality.

It may well be that civilization is only skin-deep, a veneer on the instincts of the jungle. Certainly the history of twentieth-century wars, Nazi crematoria, Russian prisons, and imperialist persecutions presents a dismal record. Nevertheless, civilization is an attempt to improve human behavior.

The standards of desirable behavior that civilization tries to establish are too high for most human beings to maintain. But the effort to maintain these standards is worth making. It is better to feel guilty about one's failure to behave well than not even try to behave well. Attempting to conceal these failures, human beings say and do hypocritical things. Paradoxically, some of this hypocrisy makes the interactions of human beings function more smoothly. Hypocrisy is one of the mechanisms indispensable for the survival of imperfect human beings in civilized society.

NOTES

Chapter One

[1]Garrett Hardin, *Bulletin of Atomic Scientists* 28:6 (June), pp. 37-41.

Chapter Two

[1]Heinrich Heine, *Works of Prose* (N.Y.: L. B. Fischer, 1943), p. 141.

[2]The material in this paragraph and the next one was provided by Elroy R. Peterson, M.D.

[3]Candace Pert, "Neuropeptides: The Emotions and Bodymind," *Noetic Sciences Review,* Spring 1987, pp. 13-18.

[4]Daniel Golleman, *Vital Lies and Simple Truths* (N.Y.: Simon and Schuster, 1985), p. 118.

[5]*Ibid.,* pp. 58-59.

[6]*Ibid.,* pp. 21.

[7]*Ibid.,* p. 32.

[8]*Ibid.,* p. 95.

Chapter Three

[1]James Harvey Robinson, *The Mind in the Making* (N.Y.: Harper, 1921), pp. 47-48.

[2]Randall Collins and Michael Maskowski, *The Discovery of Society* (N.Y.: Random House, 1978), p. 68.

[3]Goleman, *Vital Lies, Simple Truths,* pp. 161,163.

[4]*Ibid.,* p. 191.

[5]Wilson, *Sociobiology,* p. 565.

[6]*Psychology Today,* August, 1986.

Chapter Four

[1]James Frazer, *The Golden Bough* (N.Y.: Macmillan, 1950), p. 654.

[2]Konrad Lorenz, *On Aggression* (N.Y.: Harcourt, Brace, 1966), p. 168.

[3]*Ibid.,* pp. 169-170.

[4]*Ibid.,* p. 174.

[5]Rich Dawkins, "Selfish Genes and Selfish Means," in *Mind's Eye,* edited by Douglas Hofstadter and Daniel Dennett (N.Y.: Basic Books, 1981), pp. 122-123.

Chapter Five

[1]Robinson, *Mind in the Making,* p. 41.
[2]Wilson, *Sociobiology,* p. 563.
[3]*Ibid.,* p. 559.
[4]Andre Gide, *The Counterfeiters* (N.Y.: Knopf, 1962), p. 374.
[5]Marcel Proust, Maxim #130, *Maxims of Proust,* edited by Justin O'Brien (N.Y.: Columbia University Press, 1948).
[6]Phyllis Greenacre, *Swift and Carroll* (N.Y.: International Universities Press, 1955), p. 216.
[7]Charles Rycroft, *N.Y. Review of Books,* Jan. 16, 1969, p. 2.
[8]Kay R. Jamison, Study of artists and creative writers in 1983, in preparation for book on manic-depression. Reviewed in *TIME,* Oct. 8, 1984, p. 76.
[9]Ronald Hayman, *Nietzsche* (London: Wiedenfeld & Nicolson, 1980), p. 235.
[10]Harold Nicolson, *Journey to Java* (N.Y.: Doubleday, 1958).
[11]*Ibid.*
[12]Brendan Gill, *Here At The New Yorker,* (N.Y., Random House, 1975).
[13]Mary McCarthy, *N.Y. Review of Books*, Jan. 30, 1969, p. 4.
[14]Anthony Wood, quoted in footnote of Burton's *Anatomy of Melancholy,* Vol. 1, p. 106.
[15]Burton, *Anatomy of Melancholy,* Vol. 1, p. 106.
[16]Frank Muir, *An Irreverent Companion to Social History* (N.Y.: Day & Stein, 1976), p. l64.
[17]James Boswell, *Life of Samuel Johnson* (N.Y.: Oxford University Press, 1960), p. 1300.
[18]Carlin Romano, *Des Moines Register*, Sept. 11, 1986.
[19]Dale Harris, Connoisseur, June 1986, p. 82.
[20]Burton, Anatomy of Melancholy, Vol. 1, p. 61.
[21]Robinson, *Mind in the Making,* p. 46.

Chapter Six

[1]Ervin Goffman, *The Presentation of Self in Everyday Life* (N.Y.: Anchor, 1959), pp. 2,4.
[2]Wilson, *Sociobiology,* p. 576.

³Burton, *Anatomy of Melancholy,* Vol. 1, p. 466.
⁴Boswell, *Life of Johnson,* footnote on page 304.
Chapter Eight
¹Robert Barnard, *Death in a Cold Climate* (N. Y.: Scribners, 1981), p. 69.
²W. C. Allee, *Cooperation Among Animals* (N. Y.: Schuman, 1951), p. 203.
³Clark Kerr, quoted in *TIME,* Nov. 7, 1958.
Chapter Nine
¹Lorenz, *On Aggression,* p. 280.
²*Ibid.,* p. 281.
³Frederick Turner, *Des Moines Register,* July 12, 1986.
Chapter Ten
¹William Bolitho, *Twelve Against the Gods* (N.Y.: Viking Press, 1957), p. 141.
²Muir, *An Irreverent Companion . . . ,* p. 3.
³Burton, *Anatomy of Melancholy,* Vol. 1, p. 468.
⁴Bennett Cerf, *Shake Well Before Using* (N.Y.: Simon & Schuster, 1948), p. 120.
⁵George Seldes, *Witness to a Century* (N. Y.: Ballantine Books, 1987), p. 24
⁶Muir, *An Irreverent Companion . . . ,* p. 3.
⁷Hughes, *TIME,* Dec. 27, 1977.
⁸Jacques Barzun, *Harpers,* March 15, 1954, p. 44.
Chapter Eleven
¹Proust, Maxim #100.
²Bolitho, *Twelve Against the Gods,* p. 142.
³Wilson, *Sociobiology,* p. 561.
⁴Edwin Radford, *Unusual Words* (N.Y.: Philosophical Library, 1946), p. 91.
⁵Mircea Eliade, *Images and Symbols* (N.Y.: Sheed & Ward, 1961), p. 10.
⁶Robert Bocock, *Ritual in Industrial Society* (London: Allen & Unwin, 1974), pp. 143-144.
⁷Pearson, *Smith of Smiths,* p. 264.
⁸Voltaire, *Philosophical Dictionary* (N.Y.: Knopf, 1924).
⁹Ambrose Bierce, *Devil's Dictionary* (N.Y.: Dover, 1958).

[10]Heinrich Heine, *Works of Prose* (N.Y.: L. B. Fischer, 1943), p.328.
[11]New York Review of Books, July 7, 1966, p. 3.
[12]Pearson, *Smith of Smiths*, p. 325.

Chapter Twelve

[1]*Harper's*, March 1954, p. 21.
[2]Burton, *Anatomy of Melancholy*, Vol. 3, pp. 64, 65, 71.
[3]Redford, *Unusual Words*, p. 45.
[4]*Des Moines Register*, Nov. 27, 1986.

Chapter Thirteen

[1]Maurice Burton, *Animal Courtship* (N.Y.: Praeger, 1954), p. 251.
[2]Lorenz, *On Aggression*, p. 210.
[3]Irven DeVore, quoted by Edward Regis, "Dishonest Animals," *Omni*, December, 1986.
[4]*Time*, Feb. 19, 1975, p. 86.
[5]Burton, *Animal Courtship*, pp. 122-123.
[6]Wilson, *Sociobiology*, p. 353.
[7]*Ibid.*, pp. 375-377.
[8]Lorenz, *On Aggression*, p. 215.
[9]Packard, *Animal I.Q.*, p. 190.
[10]Burton, *Animal Courtship*, p. 220.
[11]Packard, *Animal I.Q.*, p. 162.
[12]Burton, *Animal Courtship*, p. 223.
[13]Frederick Drimmer, *The Animal Kingdom* (N.Y.: Greystone Press, 1954), p. 16.
[14]Lorenz, *On Aggression*, p. 201.
[15]Burton, *Animal Courtship*, p. 256.
[16]Wilson, *Sociobiology*, p. 320.
[17]Burton, *Animal Courtship*, p. 63.
[18]Drimmer, *The Animal Kingdom*, pp. 189-190.
[19]Packard, *Animal I.Q.*, p. 190.
[20]Wilson, *Sociobiology*, p. 518.
[21]Lorenz, *On Aggression*, p. 45.
[22]Lorenz, *King Solomon's Ring*, p. l52.

Chapter Fourteen

[1]J. A. B. Van Buitenen, *Tales of Ancient India* (N.Y.: Bantam Books, 1961), p. 5.

[2]Edward O. Wilson, *Sociobiology* (Cambridge: Harvard University Press, 1975), p. 549.

Bibliography

Bierce, Ambrose. *The Devil's Dictionary*. N.Y.: Dover, 1958.

Bolitho, William. *Twelve Against the Gods*. N.Y.: Viking Press, 1957.

Boswell, James. *Life of Samuel Johnson*. N.Y.: Oxford University Press, 1960.

Burton, Maurice. *Animal Courtship*. N.Y.: Praeger, 1954.

Burton, Maurice. *Inside the Animal World*. N.Y.: Quadrangle, 1977.

Burton, Robert. *Anatomy of Melancholy*. N.Y.: W.J. Widdleton, 1870.

Eliade, Mircea. *Images and Symbols*. N.Y.: Sheed & Ward, 1961.

Frazer, James. *The Golden Bough*. N.Y.: Macmillan, 1950.

Goffman, Ervin. *The Presentation of Self in Everyday Life*. N.Y.: Anchor, 1959.

Goleman, Daniel. *Vital Lies, Simple Truths*. N.Y.: Simon & Schuster, 1985.

Lorenz, Konrad. *King Solomon' Ring*. N.Y.: Crowell, 1952.

Lorenz, Konrad. *On Aggression*. N.Y.: Harcourt, Brace, 1966.

Muir, Frank. *An Irreverent Companion to Social History*. N.Y.: Stein & Day, 1976.

Packard, Vance. *Animal I.Q.* N.Y.: Dial, 1950.

Pearson, Hesketh. *The Smith of Smiths*. London: Penguin, 1948.

Robinson, James Harvey. *The Mind in the Making*. N.Y.: Harper, 1921.

Wilson, Edward O. *Sociobiology*. Cambridge: Harvard University Press, 1975.

The ET Visitor's Guide to the U.S.A

A Satire by Leonard Feinberg

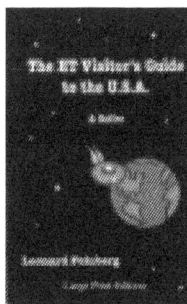

The ET Visitor's Guide to the U.S.A. is an urbane, sardonic view of American culture told from the perspective of an extraterrestrial. Like Mark Twain's *A Connecticut Yankee in King Arthur's Court* or H. L. Mencken's *Prejudices, The ET Visitor's Guide to the U.S.A.* casts a somewhat wry eye on the customs and habits of America. Entertaining and thought provoking, this satirical commentary will change forever the way you think about life in the good old US of A.

Pilgrims' Process, Inc.

4657 Huey Circle
Boulder, CO 80305-6736
Peregrino@aol.com
160 pp ISBN 0-9710609-2-4

"... *if you enjoy our [human] foibles, this book will keep you chuckling from cover to cover.*" G. S., La Jolla, CA

"*I found the early chapters a reminder of Will Rogers—short humorous jabs at the human condition.*" W. W., Highland Park, IL

"*I read, reread, laughed, chuckled, thought, rethought, and lost myself completely.*" A. K., Baldwin City, KS

"*How can you call it satire when it's true?*" D. N., Ames, IA

www.ingramcontent.com/pod-product-compliance
Lightning Source LLC
Chambersburg PA
CBHW031835090426
42741CB00005B/254